HARMONY

AND

LIGHT

HARMONY
AND
LIGHT

*10 Meditations for a
Peaceful and Purposeful Life*

WINSTON A. WARDLAW

Whisper Hints Publishing
Washington, D.C.

Whisper Hints Publishing
PO Box 5498
Washington, DC 20016
(202) 291-1231

The information presented in this book is the author's opinion
as of the date of publication and does not constitute any
replacement for health or medical advice. The content of this
book is not intended to diagnose, treat, cure, or prevent any
condition or disease. Seek guidance from a doctor or qualified
professional before beginning any new activity.

Library of Congress Control Number: 2025912471

ISBN: 979-8-9929823-0-5 (paperback)

First printing edition 2025.

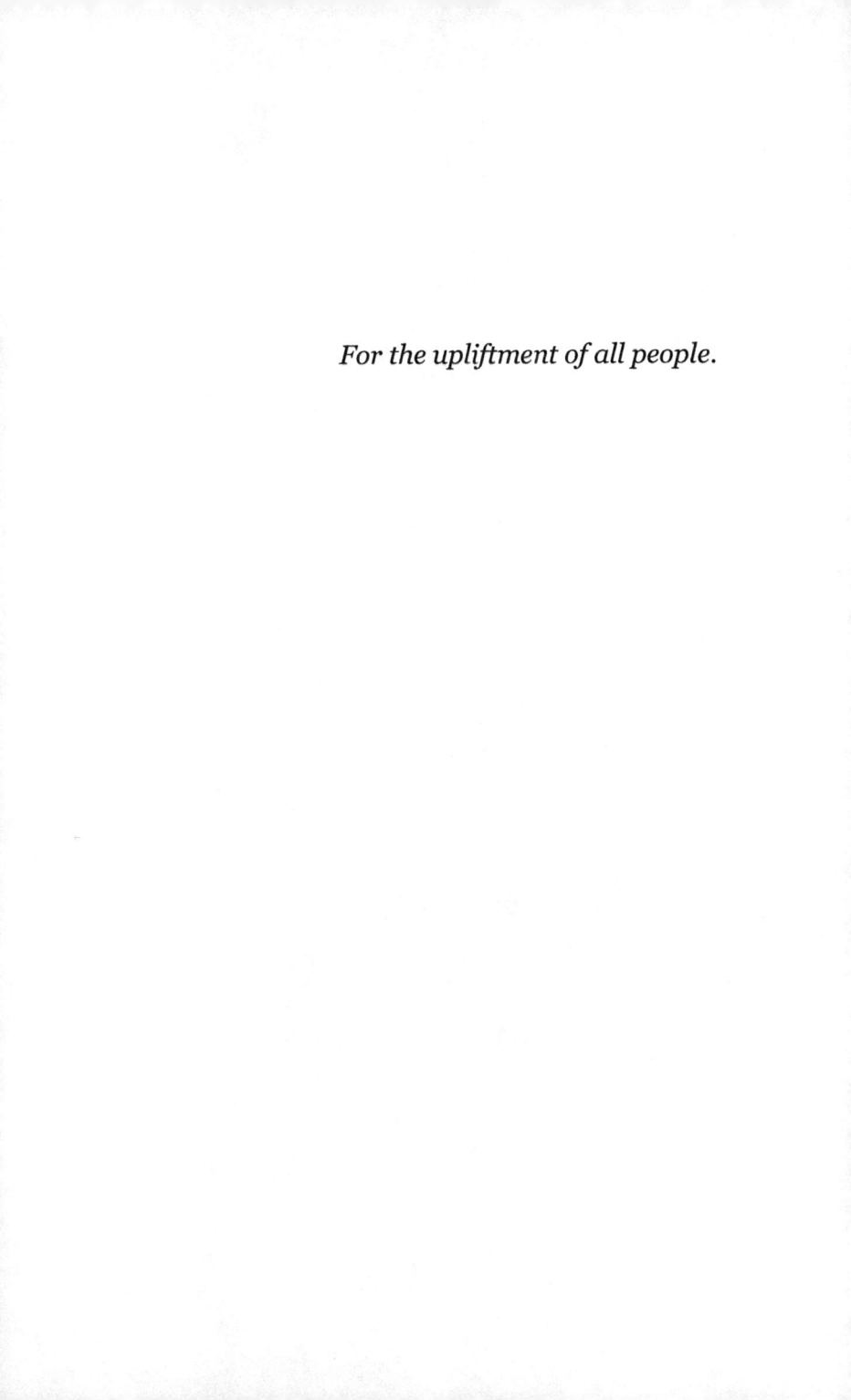

For the upliftment of all people.

*For the well-being of those who aspire
to live peacefully and purposefully.*

Acknowledgements

I wish to thank my Mom, Dad, and brother Julian for reading and providing thoughtful suggestions on my drafts, and my Uncle Chris for his cover art and interior book design suggestions. I am also appreciative of the family and friends who encouraged the writing and production of *Harmony and Light: 10 Meditations for a Peaceful and Purposeful Life*.

Contents

Introduction

In 2015, I was 12 years old, living a life that I look back on now and recognize as an example of carefree. I went to schools with kind teachers, took Tae Kwon Do classes, biked around with friends, had soccer practice after school, attended church with family members, and went to family reunions, all with the only true requirement being for me to be the best kid I could be.

During that year, I also faced situations where I felt accosted by the words of the adults around me. At that time, I lived as a perfectionist with the desire for my performance in many activities to be flawless. Whenever I felt this desire wasn't being fulfilled, I not only beat myself up with negative self-talk, but also experienced the critiques, yelling, and criticism of my performance from the adults around me as if I was being attacked. The perpetual mental stress of feeling "under attack" kept me tense and trapped me in a fight-or-flight state, which deeply affected my psyche at that age.

One afternoon I began to feel an irregular pain in my abdomen, a perpetual sensation that led to a trip to the ER. After the doctors passed off the pain as constipation, they sent me home. However, extreme agony that would force me to the bathroom and a deluge of blood that left my body whenever I used the bathroom led to two more trips to the ER.

After speaking with the front desk in the ER, on the third trip, my mother and I sat down in one hallway of the hospital, and to our surprise, a pediatric surgeon, who happened to be a parent from my brother's soccer team, came walking down the same hall. Our encounter facilitated our introduction to a prominent GI doctor who shortly thereafter provided a medical diagnosis of ulcerative colitis (UC), an autoimmune disease that causes inflammation in the large intestine. For the remainder of the year, I took medicines to treat the condition; however, my health worsened.

For months I would be in severe pain, constantly losing blood as my digestive tract scarred and became increasingly inflamed, all while I appeared normal but slightly thinner on the outside. As the common saying goes, this was the type of pain you wouldn't wish on even your worst enemy.

On December 20th, 2016, I was admitted to the hospital where I experienced a time unique from the socially constructed ideas of normal teenage years. I found myself living in a dorm-sized room unable to leave the space with many different tubes attached to my body, needing to measure the amount of blood I was losing every few hours, unable to get fresh air or see the sun most weeks, feeling more pain, and feeling like a lab rat as the doctors kept administering different drugs for me to take.

During this time of isolation and conflict, I spent weeks in solitude as I came to realize many life lessons about getting through adversity. I also tried to make the most of my seemingly unceasing adversity by exploring my interests in video game design and learning as much as I could about the hospital and biology from the wonderful healthcare professionals around me.

The time I spent in the hospital ended up totaling 67 days, spanning from December 20th, 2016, to April 22nd, 2017. I was discharged from the hospital three times, all after major gastrointestinal surgeries. In the spring of 2017, one nurse at the hospital relayed that I was nominated to be recognized as the Honored Hero of the Washington, DC Crohn's and Colitis Foundation's Take Steps Walk for my perseverance and commitment to helping other patients in the hospital with UC. I gladly accepted the invitation and delivered a 20-minute speech about my story and navigating conflict to hundreds of participants at the event.

Out of the hospital, I had slowly returned to demanding high-level competitive soccer in 2018; however, I still sometimes experienced life in a way where I was internalizing stress and feeling bombarded by the actions and words of the adults around me. Around this time, the recurrence of old symptoms of abdominal pain and a coincidental encounter with a family friend who suggested I visit a doctor who practices naturopathic medicine led to a journey of deeper understanding of health.

Soon I began to develop an awareness of the interdependence between the health of the mind, body, and spirit. As I began to meditate and learn more about the nature of life, my own life began to transform for the better. Before I gained firsthand experiences with the therapeutic approaches of holistic medical philosophies, I only knew medicine to be the use of drugs and surgery.

In my case of being diagnosed with UC, the initial therapeutic approach that was followed was to use drugs that inhibited my body's production of substances that produce inflammation in my large intestine. During the one-year span that I took these drugs, I would sometimes not present UC symptoms; however, there was no overall improvement.

By the end of the same year, I needed to receive an immediate blood transfusion due to my debilitated physical state. For this reason, I was admitted to the hospital, and the doctors worked to get me back to a state where I was more physically stable.

Upon review of some tests that were run, the doctors found that I had an infection called a *C. diff* infection. I received antibiotics (medicine that kills *C. diff* bacteria) and a common steroid prescribed to patients with UC, and my condition was further monitored. After the *C. diff* infection was gone but the flare (worsening of disease) was not subsiding, the doctors advanced me to an immunosuppressive drug to control the inflammation in my large intestine.

In my case, the medicine, even at an increased dosage delivered through a PICC line (a tube that delivers medicine directly to the large central veins near your heart), proved ineffective at establishing health in my body. I was losing a significant amount of blood every few hours and required multiple blood transfusions (my dad even donated his blood), so the doctors ultimately recommended I undergo surgery to remove my large intestine and reconstruct my digestive tract. In total I underwent three successful major gastrointestinal surgeries that would ultimately result in the creation of an internal J-pouch that would replace my large intestine and lead to a journey of adjusting to a new digestive tract. My abdomen would now have five scars resulting from two large incisions and three small incisions made during these surgeries.

Our family was grateful to have the ability to afford the comprehensive health insurance that covered my hospital stay, medical procedures, and acute health needs. We are keenly aware that this was a major blessing. I am also grateful for all the nurses' and medical doctors' love and care and for taking time to teach me so much about health, medicine, and the hospital. They all worked from their hearts to use the best tools in their medical toolkits for the purpose of helping me out, which was a blessing. As my journey continued out of the hospital, my encounter with the natural medicine doctor came at the perfect time, because I was beginning to grow interested in learning how to prevent future health bouts and how I could heal myself using approaches other than surgery and drugs.

∞∞∞∞

The firsthand experiences that I had with more natural and energy-focused medical practices helped expand my mind to view my past health problems with new perspectives.

The UC that I experienced was a condition in which the physical, mental, and spiritual aspects of my life were in a state of disharmony, and the impact of this disharmony was being expressed by my diseased large intestine. The doctors wanted to address this disharmony by treating its symptoms. From personal experience, however, I saw that utilizing allopathic medicine and only working to suppress symptoms, by themselves, are incomplete actions towards the goal of creating health.

Health is not just the absence of physical pain or unwanted symptoms; it is an expression of harmony in many aspects of our lives, and when we can begin to live with a balanced mind, body, and spirit, we will reap the great benefits of harmony.

In alignment with the nature of health being an expression of harmony within our lives and with the goal to create a healthier world, I share personal writings in this book about 10 meditations that helped me establish harmony in my life and live peacefully and purposefully throughout the conflict of my early-life health journey, even though I might not have been consciously aware of all these meditations at the time.

Conflict takes many different forms, and it can move us away from a state of harmony in our minds or spirits. However, we all have the potential to change this. We can establish harmony, even when we are dealing with conflict.

The 10 meditations in this book are intended to serve as potential sources of light that can illuminate ways to do this – ways to establish harmony so we all can live more peaceful and purposeful lives.

Harmony and Light

10 Meditations for a Peaceful and Purposeful Life

1

Self-image

*A formless self-image expands the
possibilities in our lives.*

During my early teenage years, there were many times when the importance of "believing in yourself" was explained to me while dealing with life challenges. Whether I was at school trying to learn a new subject or at a soccer practice learning a new skill, the adults around me always seemed to mention it. I appreciated the positive ideas surrounding this message at the time; however, it sometimes felt incomplete.

When I began my medical journey with UC and developed a debilitating physical state at age 13, this "believe in yourself" message felt empty, as it seemed inapplicable. Who was this "self" that I was supposed to believe in? Was it a sick person with

UC? Was it a Black boy with UC? In retrospect, it was going through this eventful health journey that helped me learn who "I" was and helped me to feel like the phrase was complete.

Knowledge of self is important. Without a solidified understanding of our self-image, meaning the concept of who we are, any positive or motivational words that we hear will just be positive and motivational words. These words might fly through our ears because these words by themselves might not always have enough power to truly catalyze the positive change we hope to see in our lives.

Before we say that we can do something, we have to recognize who our "self" is. Without doing so, our efforts to improve can seem futile. This occurrence can be observed when we try to improve ourselves physically, mentally, or emotionally, but haven't yet identified the "self" that we are trying to improve.

We are introduced to some astute stimuli, get motivated, sometimes act upon this motivation, and many times go right back to being the way we were prior to our initial motivation. We then often resign, concluding that navigating certain life challenges or achieving certain goals are insurmountable tasks. This can be a repetitive cycle of constantly being motivated and then returning to our old ways.

While exerting effort, maintaining a positive outlook on life, and believing in ourselves are extremely helpful, they by themselves cannot surpass any barriers that might be set up from a self-image associated with some "thing."

No matter the extent of positive thinking or believing in ourselves, if our inherent self-image is that of a victim, wrongdoer, failure, untouchable, inferior, or sick person, then we will be just that—a victim, wrongdoer, failure, untouchable, inferior, or sick person who also tries to use effort, think positively, and believe in themselves. In the end, the potential for positive attainment of goals can be determined by the hidden aspect of a self-image barrier.

However, by choosing to acknowledge our self-image to be that which is formless and limitless, our potential to navigate life challenges and achieve what we want to achieve can be enormously enhanced. In this way, our self-image does not needlessly limit us. This is due to the fact that our self-image forms a boundary circle around our lives.

To better understand this, it is important to know about three types of people:

1. For many of us, who establish our inherent self-image as something inferior, this circle is very

small, and its presence is then seen by the limiting effect that it can have on our lives.

2. To some people, those who establish their inherent self-image as something grand, like royalty, alpha types, "chosen ones," of great pedigree, or naturally gifted, the circle stretches a great distance; however, it is still present.

3. For only a few people, the circle is unique because it is completely absent. This is because those people know about the importance of self-image. By reaffirming their self-image as no one "thing," meaning that which is formless and limitless, they come to be known as "formless people."

While it is important that we acknowledge, honor, and educate ourselves about our physical identities in regards to the unique successes and failures of our ancestries, we should also consider making an effort to understand the quality of our identity that comes before this physical identity. And that aspect of ourselves that comes before our physical identity is our self-image. It is immaterial, but it is powerful.

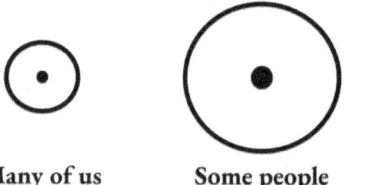

Many of us　　**Some people**　　**Formless people**

When our inherent self-image is some one "thing," whether it be of an inferior person or a superior person, an inevitable circle will form around our life. This is because when we associate ourselves with a "thing," we become bound and limited to the meaning of whatever that "thing" is.

If that "thing" is an inferior person, the circle of potential presents itself as stretching only as far as whatever an inferior person is normally capable of doing.

Similarly, if the "thing" is a superior person, this circle will only stretch as far as whatever superior people can normally do. A self-image of some superior "thing" might influence us to think we are already perfect or superior to others. This type of self-image requires us to constantly feel pressure to prove and defend our superior self-image. Such qualities might form a type of boundary or limitation around our life in the form of a detrimental stubbornness when we actually need help, an inability to embrace beneficial change, or a limited ability to express compassion.

Inferior people disempower themselves, while superior people wield the illusion of power. In both cases of inferior and superior self-images, the potential to handle life's many changing situations can in some way be limited by concepts, such as meaning, implications, or history, that all represent the "thing" being associated with the self-image. When we face challenges from this context, we might try thinking positively or believing in ourselves to help us with our problems. However, we can still be limited by whatever our self-image is, because if the challenge appears beyond the circle's boundary, there is less potential to overcome it.

When our inherent self-image becomes no one "thing" or that which is formless and limitless, circles disappear, which is what happens around the lives of *formless people*. By being formless, the absent circular barrier is devoid of any capability to impose inhibitory limitations on *formless people*.

They can become anything that is needed for the moment while still maintaining their inherently formless and limitless nature. In class, those who are formless are able to assume the mind of a student. While on the field, they become athletes. In the service shop, they transform into mechanics. On the farm they become farmers. When duty calls, they can become virtuous leaders.

While proceeding through any undertaking, they can become fully involved with and adaptive to the situation, because the formless self-image of the *formless people* allows them to have limitless potential to successfully navigate whatever the moment calls for. When these individuals are faced with a challenge or want to create some type of positive change in their lives, they can do so naturally.

Without a fixed self-image as any one "thing," *formless people* can more easily recognize there is no boundary that limits their potential to navigate any situation they face.

Throughout life, people assign an image to others, and then this image winds up becoming associated with their "self." This practice can make it easier to categorize the world we experience, and it can also be important for understanding our own unique human experiences in the context of the histories, cultures, and contemporary situations that all people have. However, for many of us, this practice in excess creates the circle that becomes a boundary and limitation for navigating our life challenges. While it might be harder to control society and stop others from assigning fixed images in our own lives, we can at least stop excessively telling ourselves that our self-image is just some one "thing."

We all have the ability to choose the self-image we want to assign to our lives and we can choose that self-image to be formless and limitless.

∞∞∞∞

Throughout my difficult experience with UC, the image that some could associate with me was a picture of being sick, weak, and forced to be isolated from others. While it is true that my body experienced these things, it was only by not associating these physical experiences with my self-image, by the way I thought and spoke, that would prevent the circular enclosure from developing.

I learned that my own personal self-image was truly formless and could not be tainted by the very real physical experiences I was going through. To affirm this formless self-image, it was important for me to recognize the common, yet silent, words and phrases that either my peers would use, or I would think, that inadvertently created the self-image boundary.

Saying phrases like "I am sick," "I am helpless," or "I am suffering from my health condition" would fortify the boundary. When peers would say, "I'm sorry to hear you are sick," this boundary would also be reinforced. What was unique about all these phrases were the words "I am" and "you are." These are phrases that often form the self-image boundary because they involve a sense of permanency. When we repeat or commonly hear these types of words, they become building blocks for the very boundary that can limit our potential to achieve things or to heal.

By learning about the beneficial implications of maintaining a formless self-image in the face of life challenges, I could actively take a mental note that my self-image was not inherently bound to all the true and severe health challenges I was going through. In essence, they were no longer character-istics of my self-image but were aspects of my living experiences. In this way, my self-image didn't be-come fixed as some "thing," like a sick boy.

This act of recognizing and affirming the challenges I was going through as experiences rather than as permanent illustrations of my self-image helped me physically, mentally, and emotionally. Being sick can often be associated with a restricted body, a resentful attitude, and depressive emotions. From this basis, there is inherently less potential to navigate the challenge of being a child in the hospital or healing from intensive surgeries.

However, by not limiting my entire self-im-age to being sick, I was not restricted by it. My self-image remained more formless and limitless, which removed the circular boundary of potential for me to experience life in different ways and get through this conflict. I was not sick, but I was experiencing sick-ness.

Though they might sound similar, there is a completely different message surrounding the two statements. One involves the permanency of "I am," and the other retains formless and limitless potential, because "I" is only experiencing something and not inherently that thing itself.

Although I was experiencing sickness, I could physically be a student completing middle school assignments from the hospital room, become a rookie foosball player, be a prospective doctor, and be a chess player. Mentally I could maintain an optimistic attitude about the potential revitalization of my body while accepting its diminished state. Emotionally, joy was not far past any circular boundary; I could feel joy even throughout the health challenges. Maintaining a formless and limitless self-image ensured that my communing with other people with inflammatory bowel diseases (IBD) in or out of the hospital did not lead me to create a circular boundary of my potential to live life positively because of the idea that "I am" a UC patient and so my life would be limited to whatever the potential of a UC patient is.

Since being sick was not my entire self-image, I could involve myself in different activities, stay optimistic, feel joy, and tap into the power necessary to overcome the challenges associated with my health journey.

If my self-image was only some one "thing," i.e., "being sick," then those activities might instead have been beyond the limitation of the circular boundary. For this reason, it was the formless and limitless self-image that helped me successfully navigate the experience of health challenges that I underwent.

∞∞∞

Throughout the day we can practice speaking and thinking differently to reaffirm the formless self-image that can dissolve the sometimes imperceptible circular boundary we might have limiting our lives. By identifying our self-image with something beyond our physical body and identifying with the quality of being formless and limitless, we can change bounded phrases like, "*I am* incapable of," or "*I am* sick and angry," to fluid phrases like, "*I am experiencing* challenges with," and "*I am experiencing* sickness and anger." We create what we speak.

The acknowledgment of life events as experiences, contrary to fixed and inherent qualities of ourselves, accurately supports the formless fluidity of our self-image. Since challenges, or any events for that matter, are acknowledged as experiences, the potential to successfully make it through them is not confined by that hidden circular boundary.

Maybe we come from backgrounds where we don't see a lot of success in certain areas of life, have physical challenges that make possibilities for peace seem remote, are put in a box by society, or have never seen anyone "like us" do "it" before. Whatever the circumstance, as long as we emphasize our inherent formless and limitless self-image and don't perpetuate ideas or self-talk that is limiting or creating a circular boundary, we will always have the ability to change our life experience. This is because our self-image won't become a "thing."

Isn't our self-image supposed to only be one thing? Is being formless even possible? Nature's guidance to *formless people* is, "The only thing in life that is permanent is change."

Embodying a formless self-image is harmonized with life's only true constant, change. We can always change. We can always grow. Every time we think and speak from the framework of "experiencing" life events, we reassure our formless nature and let go of any circular hindrances that promote a sense of permanency.

When our self-image becomes formless and changeable, we naturally become the ultimate reflection of life. In this way, our capacity to positively traverse life's undertakings is limitless.

Whenever we are experiencing difficult times in our lives, we should always believe in ourselves, and this self that we should believe in is our inherently formless self-image that is filled with limitless potential to change! *"A formless self-image expands the possibilities in our lives."*

PUTTING IT INTO PRACTICE

- *Recreate and redefine your "self-image" to become formless.*

- *Know that you aren't limited by your past or pedigree. They might be influences on your life, but they aren't the essence of who you are.*

- *Think about the words you say or think after saying "I am" and ask yourself if these words create a limitation in your life (e.g., "I am just an athlete" or "I am not good at that").*

- *Speak, think, and live in a way that embraces the limitlessness of a formless self-image.*

2

Perspective

*Our perspective gives us the power to fully
control our experience of life.*

It has been documented that the Kamba tribe in eastern Africa sees rain as the saliva of God and thus feels blessed when it lightly rains. Our auntie, planning the annual family cookout, sees rain as a nuisance and thus feels upset when it rains. Some children see snow on the ground and feel excited because they can now build a snowman. Some adults see snow on the ground and feel annoyed because now they must go outside in the cold to shovel the walk. Some people see pain as a great teacher and are thus excited to learn from it. Other people see the same pain as a great misfortune and are thus saddened when pain occurs.

While there is no difference in the events themselves, our perceptions of the events can vary greatly. It is perspective that dictates our experience of an event, not the event itself. Throughout my health journey, perspective became the central influence in how I came to experience life.

The process of identifying and categorizing life in a dualistic fashion (where life is divided into opposing realities, i.e., good or bad) is perpetuated when we are younger. It is during this time that we are taught words and meanings about various things that help tell us more about the world we live in. Things we see in our lives now have specific names. After having specific names, they also have descriptions. After having descriptions, they also have categories.

A result of this process is that words and concepts are often polarized to create categories composed of dualities. There is "healthy or unhealthy," "aced a test or failed a test," "made the shot or missed the shot," "gained or lost," "recognized or not recognized," etc. One side becomes all positive while the other is all negative. We strive for the former and try to avert the latter.

As we walk the tightrope between these extremes, usually aiming for our idea of the perfect positive, we try as hard as we can to go one way but are sometimes moved in a different direction. We thus become subject to life events and often only experience them in a dualistic fashion, with life either being a negative or positive experience.

Even though the names and descriptions of things might be presented in a positive-negative dualistic manner, we have full autonomy to experience life beyond this. When our thinking processes are stilled and we don't excessively attach ourselves to the words and definitions of things, we are able to see life as it is. This is liberation.

Since words and definitions are things we utilize to try and describe life, they by themselves cannot always completely capture the fullness of life. If our minds are too occupied with words and definitions, then we might have a difficult time experiencing life's fullness, thus getting trapped in duality.

Conversely, stilling our thinking process and beginning to perceive life from a non-dual perspective can allow for an otherwise negatively defined or categorized thing to be experienced positively. We can then choose to experience life events beyond the normal dualistic way where we get stuck in a negative or positive realm.

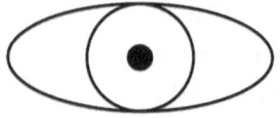

There are many times in life when it appears that we have little to no control over major circumstances affecting our lives. This was true for my family and I back in December of 2016. I found myself situated in Children's National Hospital for many weeks.

This was a time that required extensive medical procedures to treat my condition. I wasn't allowed to eat any food or leave my hospital room for many days, and I'll just say they don't keep you there unless you have to be there.

I think many people would initially assume that I entered into an unfortunate and negative situation. But from this apparently negative situation, I met some amazing people. People who will be important to my life forever. I developed a greater appreciation for family and health. I was able to take advantage of the 24/7 opportunities to learn invaluable information from dedicated doctors and nurses. I began a journey that led me to ask big questions at a young age, like, "What is the meaning of life?" I learned about perspective and how it relates to our life experience.

Perspective helped me see that although we may not always have the power to immediately change our life circumstances, the power we do have lies within our ability to choose how we experience it all.

The dualities of good or bad and positive or negative truly exist in the perspectives from which we choose to view our lives. The way I experienced all the circumstances I was going through in the hospital was dictated by how I chose to look at them.

If I were to say that being in the hospital is only a positive experience, it wouldn't be completely true. But if I were to say that being in the hospital is only a negative experience, it also wouldn't be true. In both cases, I would be playing the ultimate game of self-deception.

The truth is that the hospital is just the hospital. Nothing more, nothing less. How I chose to perceive the state of being in the hospital, which directly affected my experience of it, was completely up to me. The hospital is what you make of it.

Similarly, rain is just rain. The Kamba tribe holds the perspective of rain being full of blessings, while our auntie planning the family cookout has the perspective of rain being a curse. It might be the exact same type of rain for both of them, but their experiences on a rainy day will be completely different because their experience is ultimately shaped from within.

∞∞∞

The vast and starry night sky above reminds us that the universe is infinite. Just as it is infinite above, so can the depth of our experience of life be here below on earth.

Regardless of whatever seemingly negative or positive circumstance we are going through, our perspective of it gives us an inexhaustible capacity to experience life in any way that we'd like. Our perspective thus serves as a natural confirmation that our experience of life truly happens from within. When we are able to view all life events as possibilities to experience a new dimension of life as opposed to being subject to experiencing the fixed polarities of good or bad, our lives naturally become a journey.

When we begin to intentionally choose how we want to perceive the world, we can become masters of our life experience. Disease can be appreciated as a signal from the body telling us what dietary, environmental, career, or lifestyle changes we need to make to live a more balanced life. Past mistakes we made can be seen as a wonderful gift that allows us to understand what aspects of our character we can look to refine. Times of solitude can be viewed as a chance to look within ourselves and rest our minds.

A wise person once said, "Sometimes we think we made a wrong turn, but it ends up being the right turn we needed to make to get to where we need to be." Everything, in the end, comes down to perspective throughout our life journeys.

Freedom lies within our ability to only give control of our life experience to ourselves, and not to anybody or anything outside of us. This is how we can empower ourselves greatly.

A life challenge is only a challenge because we choose to view it that way, and a life opportunity is only an opportunity because we choose to view it as such. *"Our perspective gives us the power to fully control our experience of life."*

PUTTING IT INTO PRACTICE

- *Choose your own experience of life.*

- *Let go of ideas and concepts that limit you to seeing life from a fixed/dual point of view (e.g., good or bad).*

- *Practice thinking and speaking from a non-dual point of view.*

- *Look at life circumstances and events as opportunities.*

3

Gratitude

*Gratitude brings us back to our original
undisturbed state of peace.*

When a full dinner meal has been prepared and is ready to eat, our desires are fulfilled as our stomachs gain a succulent meal. Once we finish the meal, though, we lose the feeling of tasty food in our mouth, and we can find ourselves desiring more.

Whether it is food, friends, status, or money, the process of gaining and losing is the natural rhythm of life. Unfortunately, the experiences of gain and loss can become undesirable when they seem to involve conflict in our lives. But there is a way to address this conflict. We can learn to live perfectly through both gain and loss by cultivating gratitude.

To understand gratitude, we first must know about the main culprit for its absence, *desire*. It is natural to aspire to live a pleasant life with the time we have on this earth, since it is a brief spark of time. However, when we develop untamed desires for something we don't have in life, these desires often exceed our gratitude for reality as it is, and we can suffer.

When we desire more, we suffer while being reminded that we aren't, or don't have, enough. The more we desire to change the past, the more we constantly are reminded that life only moves forward while we suffer through our futile efforts to go back. The more we desire to be on top, the more we suffer because there is always something higher while we endlessly climb up. The more we desire to hold onto things, the more we suffer when we are without things. The more we desire to control the world, the more we are reminded that the world is bigger than us, so we suffer from our lack of control.

In all cases, continued desire leads to a more incomplete life, where we think life will only be complete when our desires are being fulfilled. Naturally, we aspire for our life to feel as though it is complete, since "complete" seems perfect. However, because of the incompleteness perpetuated by our desires, perfection is constantly being lost, and we suffer while trying to get it back.

As the time spent living in this incomplete life increases, the state of our suffering will also increase, and we can become prisoners of our rich tastes. There is a way out of this, though.

In comparison to desire, gratitude emphasizes life's completeness. Gratitude helps us recognize what is already beautifully in our lives, making our lives complete. Constantly living in a complete world helps bliss become our natural state because life is perfect as it is.

The more we cultivate our gratitude for the little things in life, the more we can understand true meaningfulness and value. The more we are grateful for the blessings of the present, the less ideal changing or dwelling in the past appears, because it might have postponed the self-cultivation we need or needed to go through. The more gratitude we express for being lower, the more we recognize that being higher is less stable. The more gratitude we have for loss, the more lessons we learn about the suffering that is often caused by gain. The more gratitude we have for life as it is, the less we suffer feeling like we have to always change it.

Oftentimes we overlook the little, seemingly unimportant, things in life because they seem useless. However, it is *valuing* these very little and seemingly unimportant things that is often the very nature of gratitude. By curbing our desires and cultivating a state of gratitude, we can live a more peaceful life.

Gratitude and desire played central roles in the peace and suffering I experienced throughout my own health journey. There were some hours in the hospital when I would not experience extreme pain, which allow me free time. Other hours I would experience agonizing abdominal pain, which led to frequent trips to the bathroom to release blood from my digestive tract. During those frequent hours of agony, I desired change, for all the pain to be gone, to not have to deal with the debilitating nature of UC, and to be healthy.

I desired to change the past and questioned if my challenging circumstances would not have occurred if I had done something differently. What if I had not cared so much about being a perfectionist? What if I was just "normal?" What if I didn't overthink everything? What if I didn't beat myself up with negative self-talk? What if I had not eaten so much Halloween chocolate candy before being diagnosed with UC?

In this process of desiring change, I felt powerless, small, scared, and as though life was incomplete. I suffered this way.

While the days passed in the hospital, my life became rhythmic. It involved regular repetitions of being with or without pain and gaining or losing strength. Throughout these cycles, I developed a great sense of gratitude whenever the good times were there. I felt at ease and blissful during these times because life felt complete. However, when the bad times came back and my desires for change sometimes grew, my gratitude diminished, and I would suffer.

After my first surgery to remove my large intestine, I was informed that one of my new friends in the hospital had recently undergone the same surgery, and that upon removal her colon was even more inflamed than mine had been. This was shocking news to me, as I couldn't fathom how much more pain she might have been in than me. At this time, many of my desires decreased as I developed great gratitude for the challenging, yet sparing, situation I was going through. I felt more at peace with life because it didn't feel so incomplete.

A little while after this, when I was discharged from the hospital for the third and final time, I was feeling great. I had gratitude that my desires had been met, since I was finally liberated from the hospital and allowed to come back home. However, as the weeks passed while recovering, and I remained at home or near a bathroom often, I began to strongly desire to live a life more similar to my peers.

As these desires (like playing soccer again, going on long car rides, socializing with peers, or doing whatever I thought was "normal" for kids my age) increased and overshadowed my gratitude, my suffering also increased because these desires were not being met. This left my life feeling incomplete. Even after my main desire to be out of the hospital was met, my life could still become incomplete because new desires would arise and dominate my mind as I drifted away from gratitude. Desire was blinding me, and my joy would depend on the chance of my external circumstances being a specific way.

As the weeks passed, I constantly would cycle between feeling gratitude for the times I had good digestion and feeling desire for my life to be normal, whatever I thought that was at the time. However, one afternoon after a notably challenging morning of constantly needing to use the bathroom and being tired from loose bowel movements, something changed. Even with a weak body and an incomplete digestive tract that was burdening my body, my desires dissolved. I found myself expressing gratitude for my breath while I focused on each breath I took. I was grateful for my legs and would focus on each step. I was grateful for my hands and focused on every movement I made. I was grateful for the sunlight and cherished the warm coat it gave my skin. I was grateful for the stillness caused by tough times in life that would humble me and help me see beauty even during undesirable times. This meditative process of expressing gratitude for all of life let me naturally experience a state of serenity.

Eventually, when good things happened in my life, I would express gratitude for life. In the same fashion, when bad things happened, I would still also express this gratitude. My mind rested in an optimistic attitude. Desires for change wouldn't easily overshadow my gratitude for life, and my peace was maintained throughout the highs and lows. With gratitude, I accepted life as it came to me. With gratitude, my internal peace was beyond gain or loss.

∞∞∞

To the degree that we can't tame our desires, we can suffer. Similarly, to the degree that we cultivate gratitude, the more naturally we can progress through life while living in an undisturbed state of peace. There is always something in life we can find gratitude for, always something that can remind us life is already complete the way it is. When we actively remind ourselves of this, the bliss that is accompanied by gratitude can be felt all throughout life.

To cultivate our gratitude, we can also meditate on the teaching that less is more and more is less. Less untamed desire can allow for more gratitude and more feelings of completeness. Comparably, more untamed desire can create less gratitude and less of a feeling of completeness. By working towards our goals while also expressing gratitude for life, we can actively work towards goals without stretching away from life and being a slave to the effort of creating a complete life that is only made by fulfilling some excessive desire.

It is often the easy path of accepting life as it comes and letting things take their natural course that seems harder, while the harder path of trying to attain all our many changing desires seems easy. We might find displeasure in having less or being in unfavorable situations; however, these times in life need not disrupt our peace. When big, small, favorable, or unfavorable things happen, we can always actively express gratitude for some aspect of life. This way we can maintain our undisturbed state of peace.

Maintaining gratitude through all situations can help us recognize that all life experiences can be meaningful in their own way and that life never truly loses its perfect completeness. By expressing gratitude throughout both gain and loss in our lives, we have the opportunity to begin experiencing perfect living: peace beyond gain or loss. *"Gratitude brings us back to our original undisturbed state of peace."*

PUTTING IT INTO PRACTICE

- *Reflect on the day and write down 1-5 things you are grateful for before bed each night.*

- *Let go of your untamed desires and accept life as it comes.*

- *Practice letting gratitude become the natural state of your mind.*

- *Find appreciation for simple things.*

4

Joy

Being joyful lets us fly through life.

B efore the end of the academic year in elementary school, teachers would always leave two messages with the children. First, they would say, "Hope you enjoy the summer break," and second, "The time will fly by." These comments hold true for many kids because during the summer they are in a constant state of joy, and by the end of summer, time seems to have flown by.

As we get older and go on road trips with close friends or family, a similar experience happens. One second the travel time on the GPS says three hours, and seemingly the next second it only shows 45 minutes. All the laughs, smiles, and fun conversations seemed to make the time fly by.

While it often seems that the time itself is flying by, my health journey helped me learn that time itself never actually flies. Instead, it is us who do this flying, and when we take time to observe the flying creatures of the world, we can learn to fly naturally just like them.

One of the most fascinating animals in the world is the eagle. Born with wings and light bones, these creatures were gifted with the ability to soar through the sky. Every day they gracefully flap their wings, traveling up, down, left, and right as they traverse the endless sky. Since they carry a light load, they are never weighed down by unnecessary baggage that would otherwise burden their wings. They stay light and fly.

Just as these birds dance through the sky with their light load and wings stretched wide, we too can do the same. When we are joyful, we become just like the eagles who are spreading their wings. While some emotions like depression, worry, or sadness tend to be heavy emotions and weigh us down, joy is light. Joy supports our stretched-out wings that are flying us through life.

Sometimes life may be rough or scary, and sometimes there are hardships. However, we still always have our wings with us, and by being joyful, these wings can fly us through these circumstances.

With a lighter load, we can have a pleasant flight that makes the journey smoother and avoid the heavy load that would keep us weighed down closer to the ground, hindering our travel. Our joy might even be so contagious that it helps other people living with a heavy load become light so they too can fly.

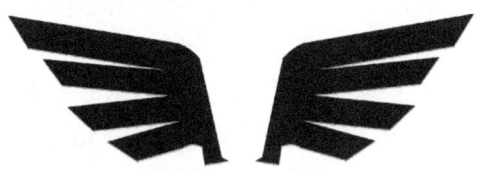

A common question we may ask during any difficult situation we are in is, "When will I get out of this hardship?" We ask this during those heavy times when we feel burdened, attached, or restricted by the difficulties in our lives.

This held true for my family when I was discharged from the hospital and my body was healing from my medical procedures. I experienced many long days and nights constantly attending to the bathroom and was met with uncertainty as to how my new digestive tract would continue to function. Additionally, there was no official timeline for when my body would get stronger after having dropped down to only 92 lbs (41 kg) in the hospital, developing stretch marks on my legs from this rapid weight fluctuation, and losing the ability to energetically walk around. This was a heavy time for my family and me, especially at age 13.

However, even through it all, we still had our wings. Our wings were always trying to let us fly, and whenever we magnified our inner joy, kept a positive outlook on life, laughed, smiled, and tried to have fun, our wings would then stretch wider and seamlessly glide us through this time.

In this way we embodied joy and became lighter, letting our wings fly us more smoothly through the day. When night came, everything would seem to have passed by so quickly. We had the choice to not always be dependent on external situations to make us joyful. Keeping a joyful demeanor was not a way to escape the heavy situation we were in, it was the assurance that our wings could still fly us tranquilly through any life situation. As we smiled and laughed with joy, we became lighter, and our wings could let us soar through the endless sky that is life's beauty.

Through this experience I was able to learn that it is all of us who do the flying, not time. We fly because we have wings, and when we all start to embrace joy, we can let these wings glide us through any circumstance we are going through.

∞∞∞∞

Every time we see a baby, we are reminded that the wings are with us, as we often look at babies as being born with wings of their own. Babies are precious to our hearts and seem to act like angels, as they lighten up our moods after a heavy day. Their contagious, uplifting presence is a result of being filled with joy. Smiling often and laughing all throughout the day, babies keep a light load as their wings glide them through the day. On the contrary, the average adult is said to laugh very few times a day. Adults often carry a heavier load, making for a more laborious life journey. We can change this, though.

Whenever we keep a joyful and positive out-going demeanor through hardship, we can fly through any challenge. Whether it be a hard class in school, career challenges, illness, setbacks in sports, or other circumstances, we always have the ability to expand our inner joy, smile, laugh, live truthfully, and spread our wings.

Joy glows from within. When we are no longer dependent on any external stimuli or situation to make us joyful, we have the opportunity to experience unlimited joy. This joy is unlimited because it comes from the limitless depths of our glowing heart. Beyond our personal life experiences, living with inner joy can also invite and attract similar joy in our external circumstances, because they will resonate with what is within our hearts.

Our wings have always been there, patiently waiting for the ideal time to fly. This ideal time is when we become light, and we become light when we are joyful. So why not embrace joy so you too can fly? *"Being joyful lets us fly through life."*

PUTTING IT INTO PRACTICE

- *Practice trying to naturally experience joy for life itself.*

- *Let go of your heavy emotional load so you can become light, spread your wings of joy, and fly.*

- *Smile, laugh, and spread positivity to others.*

- *Remember, "Life is too short to be dead serious all the time; smile."*

5

Heart

*Whatever you pour your heart into can
become something beautiful.*

When I was younger, there were talented soccer players in my neighborhood. I would
always find myself inspired by their skill and wanted
to improve on my own. Eventually, some of us
started to play pickup games together, and we began
to develop a great friendship. For hours my neighborhood friends, brother, and I would kick a soccer
ball and focus on each movement we made as we enjoyed fun adventures playing soccer at the local park.
The time we spent playing was very meaningful to
us, and we would pour our hearts into each game we
played.

It was clear then how I should live my life
whenever I was with my soccer crew: pouring my

heart into playing the beautiful game. However, when I got a little older and was secluded by spending time in the hospital for my diminished health, a big question entered my mind: "How should I live my life now?" It was during this time that I learned we do not need to pour our hearts into only one thing; we are not supposed to choose only one. Instead, we can live with a heart that pours its all into everything, just like the sun.

When the sun shines its light, it does so unconditionally. It gives seeking nothing in return, and it doesn't choose to only pour its all into one thing on earth. Ideas of importance and unimportance are not in its language. Whether it's a rose from a botanical garden in the west, a rice plant from a farm in the east, a mailman in the north, or soccer players in the south, the sun is devoted to shining onto them all.

It is by giving its all to all things that the sun helps ensure everything on earth has the potential to become something great. By shining its light onto the rose, the sun is able to help that rose blossom and make the botanical garden look like a wonderland. The sun's light ensures the rice plant will have the ability to mature and be ready for harvest, that the skin of the mailman will have the capability to synthesize Vitamin D, and that the soccer players will be able to have nice weather for a Sunday league game. All of these different things benefit from the sun's light, and the sun gives its all to each of them. If the sun were only to shine in the west, the north, south, and east would be disregarded and not realize their full potential.

This is a grand demonstration of how living with heart can create a world full of the potential for beautiful things to manifest. By embracing this demonstration of the sun, we can also create a beautiful life of our own. When we pour our hearts into everything we do, seeing the value in all things, beauty can also surround us.

When I was in my hospital room and unable to leave the small space, the scope of what I could do seemed to contract. I no longer had the ability to spend the afternoon playing soccer with my brother and friends or engage in common extracurricular activities I used to enjoy during my early adolescent years. For some time in that hospital room I mentally struggled through this hardship, as I questioned how I was supposed to live. However, this experience helped me learn that for something to contract, it often means something else expands.

After some time passed, my state of deep inquiry subsided as I became interested in all things associated with my experience in the hospital. This was something that led me to pour my heart into everything, just like the sun, whose rays lit up everything on earth, including my dark hospital room.

Whenever the doctors and nurses conducted their rotations and came into my room, I completely directed my focus towards our interactions. I tried to absorb as much information as I could from them and asked many clarifying questions from a place of sincere and motivated interest. By doing this, I was pouring my heart into the process of interacting with the healthcare professionals.

After many weeks in the hospital and countless interactions with these professionals, I was asked if I would be open to speaking with other people with UC in the hospital to share how I was navigating my health journey. With an open and devoted heart, I followed through and spoke with other children living with IBD.

These interactions continued, and eventually I was asked to serve as the Honored Hero for the Crohn's and Colitis Foundation's Washington, D.C.

Take Steps Walk. Although I never had the goal to be in such a situation, it was by pouring my heart into all aspects of my experience in the hospital with an outgoing and joyful demeanor that the potential for such an opportunity was planted. And, at the event, I stood in front of the Washington Monument and delivered a speech about my journey with UC to hundreds of participants, hoping to resurrect a sense of hope for anyone who may have been feeling down. My intention was to offer inspiration and words of encouragement to other IBD patients and their family members. I tried to emulate the sun, which glows and brightens our day even if we're having a hard time.

In addition to focusing my heart on speaking with healthcare professionals and people living with IBD, I also focused my attention on creating things during my time in the hospital. My brother and I always loved playing with building blocks and video games when we were younger; however, we weren't able to play these things the same way during my hospital stay.

Despite the extended time of inactivity within the hospital, a new thought of exploring how video games were built arose in my mind. This thought then led to time and interest being directed towards following online tutorials about creating video games. Although following these tutorials often started off as an arduous task, I poured my heart into the task with a joyful and positive outlook as I learned different aspects of video game design while in the hospital.

After a few years passed, that initial seed that had been planted from pouring my heart into creating video games grew into projects where my brother and I worked together with deep, focused, and protracted concentration and eventually published three apps for mobile devices. Similar to the Take Steps Walk, there was never an initial intention to achieve any result. Instead, it was with a joyful and devoted heart that a seed of potential could be planted for the publishing of the apps.

Since I initially felt there was not much I could do while in the hospital, I did whatever I could. And I made sure whatever I did was propelled by my whole heart. My only goal was to pour my heart into all aspects of life.

In addition to these experiences that began in the hospital, the focus of my heart expanded during the time after my final discharge, when I began to pour my heart into the more spiritual aspects of life. This focus included a motivated search for purpose and the meaning of life; however, during this search, I tried to ensure that my devotion to all things was maintained.

Whether I was sitting in a school class, cleaning my room, or focusing on personal growth, my goal was to involve myself fully in each moment. By becoming open to pouring my heart into all things, the mental hardship in my health journey, characterized by feeling stuck from not knowing how to live, was remedied.

∞∞∞∞

A crisis can sometimes happen in our lives when we feel stuck and do not know how to live. We ask, "What should I do?" "What is the point of life?" and "How am I supposed to live?" It is important to look within to realize what is meaningful to us and what makes up the purpose of our life; however, there is also great benefit in remembering to look up to remember the lessons of the sun as we live our daily lives.

We can always live with a heart that pours into all. Whether we are cleaning our rooms, speaking to neighbors, studying for classes, or working on a new soccer skill, by pouring our whole heart into each, they can all become something beautiful.

The room can be clear of clutter, which might reduce our levels of stress. The conversation with our neighbor might turn into striking a new friendship that helps build common unity. The time spent studying for a class might teach us skills that prove beneficial later in life. Practicing the skill of juggling a soccer ball might help us develop an extraordinary work ethic, something that can translate into a beneficial skill in academics or business. One of the highest expressions of living is being able to recognize our oneness with all things, and living with a devoted spirit and a heart that pours into all aspects of life lets us do just that.

Beyond the material aspects of life, there are also benefits to pouring our hearts into the immaterial, such as personal growth. Imagine a world where devotion to human development and material development are more equal. When this balance is achieved, we would no longer prioritize trying to make or gain better things while overlooking the need to make better humans, who aren't greatly controlled or excessively victimized by greed, depression, lust, envy, wrath, and other self-destructive and socially destructive tendencies.

Even with all the technological development in the world, there is still a significant prevalence of people hurting each other, themselves, and the planet. By devoting our hearts to personal development, we can work to create better people. We polish the material and immaterial facets of life when we pour our entire heart into developing both.

By actively investing our hearts in everything we do and seeing the importance in all aspects of life, we can live more like the sun and plant seeds of abundant potential in our lives. *"Whatever you pour your heart into can become something beautiful."*

PUTTING IT INTO PRACTICE

- *Pour your heart into everything.*

- *Practice trying to see the value of everything in life.*

- *Live with great passion and enthusiasm.*

6

Seasons

Everything in life goes through cycles,
and each part of every cycle serves a purpose.

During the time I spent in the hospital as a child, I was largely confined to a room that did not get direct sunlight. Although this led me to not completely see the sun for many weeks, I was able to observe an interesting phenomenon. No matter what, the sky confirmed that there was a period of darkness followed by a period of light, darkness again, and then light once more. This cosmic dance between light and dark would continue, and it demonstrated that the transitions in the sky follow a natural cycle, something our lives also follow.

From being close friends with southern U.S. farmers, I learned that farmers are very attuned to this same cyclical reality in nature. This is because their lives are centered around being in harmony with the characteristics of each season, so their farms can consistently produce palatable produce. By observing how farmers connect with the seasons, I learned that we can also live better and more balanced lives when we are able to understand the importance of seasons within our own personal journeys.

It is a futile effort for farmers to fight the season they are in. They know that trying to change or speed up to a more favorable farming season is not natural. Instead, they adjust their farming practices as if they were sailors adjusting the sails of a boat riding through changing water. During an excessively rainy period of the year, they might decrease the water supply they normally have directed towards the fields. Similarly, during an excessively dry period, they might increase this water flow. Just as my farmer friends know that adjusting their farming practices to match the current weather pattern is a necessary action for the maintenance of their fields, they also know that each season presents its own circumstances to which they must adjust.

During the season of spring, farmers know they are in for a time of planting seeds they hope will blossom into beautiful produce later in the year. The symphony of the birds, buzzing of the honeybees, and blossoms of the flowers characterize spring. All of nature embodies the characteristics of "creating." Farmers find it favorable to be connected to this period of creation as they take part in this time of new beginnings.

Summer is a season of bountiful plant growth. The longer days, warmer weather, and increased exposure to sunlight provide plants with ample time to undergo photosynthesis, the process that promotes their growth. During this time of abundant energy, farmers methodically monitor and protect their plants by ensuring they have adequate water and by removing invasive weeds. By doing so, they are working in tandem with the dynamics of the summer season to support their agricultural efforts.

Fall is the harvesting season for farmers. The weather is beginning to cool down, and the tree leaves are starting to change color due to the decrease of daylight hours. Before the leaves depart from the branches, the trees pull the nutrients from the leaves inward, storing them in the roots. This process signals to the farmers that their crops are also ready to undergo change. Crops are ripe at this time, and the farmers now pick them from the fields so they can be eaten or stored.

Lastly, winter is the season of senescence. The leaves have all fallen from the trees, and the crops have all been picked from the fields. The colors and vitality that were displayed by nature in the fall are now hidden. Winter is also a time for reflection and planning. Farmers look back on their farming methods from the previous year and make plans to enhance them in the year to come.

As the end of winter approaches, farmers experience nature's extreme state of environmental rest. Nature looks like a grayscale image; it is quieter, the ground is frozen, and the hours of sunlight are now very limited. Everything is at a standstill. In the dead of winter, when all is diminished and depleted, great farmers know that the cycle of life is not over. They do not lose hope that their fields will again be bountiful. Although they might grieve, they do not linger in grief due to nature's rest.

Being in touch with the ways of nature, they know that after the winter solstice, the day with the fewest hours of sunlight, the sun will again be born into the sky. Its birth will increase the hours of sunlight and lead all of nature to transition back into the season of spring. Life will then be reborn, and all of nature will emerge from the ground. The *will* of nature is reborn.

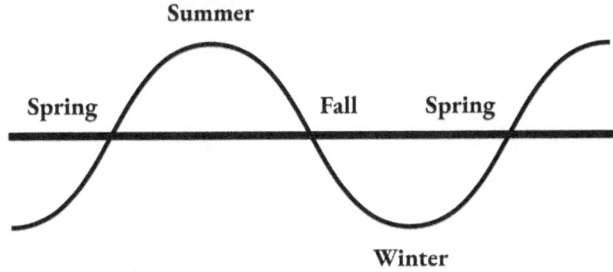

Throughout the annual cycle, nature reminds farmers not to lament the season they are in and desire change to come sooner. Over time, farmers learn to accept where life is, knowing every season of the annual cycle serves a unique purpose. If they ignored nature by planting seeds when they pleased, rather than when nature provided the adequate time and environment to do so, they would face many hardships. Without the proper temperature, humidity, and sunlight conditions, those same seeds might decompose rather than grow.

By embracing patience, farmers accept life's natural limits and observe nature's lesson that "Everything happens in time, when it's time." Within this lesson, nature consistently demonstrates that the four seasons do not rush through life, yet all things come to perfect completion by the end of the year.

Every day of the year, through the rising and setting of the sun, nature teaches the concept of cycles without trying. The sun serves as the ultimate proof of natural transitions. In the morning, the sun aspires to be bright and rise up high in the sky. However, at noon, when it reaches its zenith, it knows that now all it can do is fall. It accepts the natural change. During this descent, farmers say, "See you later," as the earth continues to rotate and the sun shines its light onto other places around the earth. Inevitably, the sun rises and shines its light back down onto the same farmers again. Everything has its day in the sun.

∞∞∞∞

As I have learned the ways of the farmer, I have been able to observe my own life and see how natural cycles were evident within it. A winter season occurred in my life when I entered the hospital. My health was diminished and my body was weak. The window of the hospital room revealed that the daylight hours were limited, and so was the personal energy I felt for extraversion.

Similar to the winter season for the farmers, this was a quiet time for me that involved deep contemplation. I didn't ask, "Why me?" or become a victim and eagerly desire for this season of my life to change. With patience and optimism, I tried to accept the season I was in and see the season through to completion while I embraced introversion. I tried to understand the importance of the season I was in. Just as plants withdraw their nutrients inwards and downwards during winter, I withdrew my focus inwards to focus on healing.

Times of spring occurred in my life the three times I was discharged from the hospital after my surgeries. During the season of spring, I was able to see the sunrise and feel the sunlight that I had missed for many days. This time was characterized by the birth of new experiences, knowledge, life skills, and increasing physical strength. My physical stagnation ceased, and a time when I wasn't bound to a hospital bed or hospital room emerged. My body transitioned into a new phase where it was adjusting to a different gastrointestinal tract, and I was slowly beginning to be able to happily spend time surrounded by close family in different spaces.

The summer season happened for me when I was able to identify foods and remedies that supported my unique body constitution and when my body became increasingly well-adjusted to my new physiology. This allowed me to go throughout the day full of energy, have better digestion, and enjoy a more extroverted life where I could engage in more of the activities that I used to do with my brother and close friends. During this season, it would feel like joy and pleasant circumstances were more prevalent around me, just like a nice summer day with a glowing sun overhead.

A fall season happened in my life when I began to slowly pull my attention inward to harvest all of the lessons that I learned and experienced over time. Harvesting these lessons allowed me to store them in my mind for the benefit of future seasons to come. During this season I would also let go of any physical things, negative emotions, or ideas that no longer had a positive purpose in my life. My extraversion would contract, and my introversion would expand so I could store and fuel up my body and mind. Through all these experiences, I learned firsthand that each season served a purpose to move me into the next phase of my life.

We do not have to go through severe winter seasons to learn and grow. However, when we do experience such times, we can benefit from knowing we have been given an opportunity for immense personal growth to occur. It is easy to match larger, more significant transitions in life with the cycles of the seasons; however, life's cycles are not limited to major events; they occur every day, just like the rising and setting of the sun.

∞∞∞∞

Without some rain, plants can't grow. If farmers wanted to quickly rush to fall to harvest their crops, but they saw no purpose in rain and wanted to force their way out of the rain, there would be no crops to harvest. Similarly, in our own lives, there are rainy times. We might feel like we messed up, missed an opportunity, or experienced loss. While it might feel like a severe storm with heavy rain, this rainy time might be the same rain that is helping to grow something beautiful in our lives.

Applying the knowledge of cycles by understanding the transformation of nature through its changing seasons can help us all better go through the changing times of our own lives. When times are rough, quiet, isolated, or feeling like a standstill, we can know that we are in a period of winter. This can signal to us that we will soon transition into spring, where we will have a time for the birth of new and different experiences. When times are good and lively, we can understand that we are in a period of summer and will soon transition into fall, where life will begin to slow down and where we should direct our attention inward to prepare for the coming quiet time of winter.

Our understanding of the ever-transforming seasons in life can also help us avoid extremes. For example, by understanding that a period of spring is

right around the corner during a difficult winter period, any excessive fear that would otherwise occur
during this difficult time is decreased. Similarly,
knowing that a period of fall comes right after a time
of summer limits any excessive infatuation with the
joy and pleasant times that might happen during a
summer period.

From this understanding of seasons in life, a
broader perspective can be used to view any situation that we are dealing with in the world, whether
wanted or unwanted. Just as farmers see the value of
each season, we can also begin to value each season
in our lives. When we trust that there is purpose to
every season, we live from a principle that is funda-
mental to nature's perfection: constant cyclical
change.

Nature is perfect because it's dynamic, and so
are our lives. We must remember that without a period of winter in our lives, there would be no birth of
spring. Without spring, there would be no expansion
of summer. Without summer, there would be no inward pull of fall. Without fall, there would be no
standstill of winter.

Whether it be nature, power, or nations, everything moves in cycles. They rise, flourish, fall, die,
and then rise again. It is natural and eternal cycles,
composed of interdependent seasons, that are the

essence of life's ability to transform from one thing to another.

As we go through periods of adversity, it can help to remember the natural, cyclical flow of nature that is ever present within our lives so we may also transform our lives. *"Everything in life goes through cycles, and each part of every cycle serves a purpose."*

PUTTING IT INTO PRACTICE

- *Relax your mind and trust the natural flow of life's cycles.*

- *Practice trying to recognize the importance of all seasons in life.*

- *Practice patience.*

7

Flexibility

Embracing flexibility nourishes our lives.

When our blood vessels are hard and not flexible, they are closer to injury. When a tree is stiff and not flexible, it is prone to snapping. When a leaf is hard and not flexible, it is close to death. When our skeletal muscles are tight and not flexible, they are likely to tear. When water is solid, it can crack, and when it is liquid, it can flow. Flexibility is associated with longevity, while inflexibility is associated with death. In alignment with this law of life, learning to become flexible was essential to overcoming the conflict I faced in my health journey.

When our lives become too fixed, we can find ourselves subject to misfortune, and for this reason, it is important to know about a central cause of inflexibility in our lives: attachment. Life is dynamic, and by holding on to things, we disrupt the vital characteristic of life that is changeability.

We can see the effects of attachment in our lives when we hold tightly to our conditionings (likes, dislikes, customs, perspectives, etc.). An unwavering attachment to conditionings is an inflexible state that can cause us to experience limitations within different aspects our lives, stiffen our lives, and move us away from longevity.

If a teacher only likes instructing their class using methods that worked many years ago when they started teaching, they might not reach their current students, who better respond to modern teaching approaches. By sticking to their likes and not being flexible in their approach, the teacher satisfies their personal attachments but might leave many students behind. In this case, they are impacting their longevity as a teacher because they have become too attached to their likes and have not embraced flexibility.

Conditioning to dislike something can result in a similar outcome. If a scientist sincerely dislikes working out because it diverts them from their fascinating experiments and they choose to only indulge in their academic pursuits 24/7, they can invite injuries due to their sedentary lifestyle. Although they might live doing what they love, making beneficial discoveries, it does not mean they are exempt from the concept of longevity, which emphasizes the flexibility of being able to balance physical movement and stillness.

Attachment to our conditioned customs might reinforce a solidified sense of identity and community; however, it might also promote inflexibility. A tradition or custom that might have beneficially served us in the past might no longer serve us in the present. In this case, recognition and being flexible by letting go of attachment is important.

An attachment to permanent perspectives might increase someone's confidence and the depth of their knowledge; however, their stone wall of solidified ideas can form an entrapment. This is similar to the limiting effects of having a fixed self-image or of not recognizing the power we have to choose and change our perspectives. A solidified self-image that isn't changeable creates an inherently limited, fixed circular boundary in our lives, and a fixed, unchangeable perspective of life limits the depth of possibility for our life experience. In both cases, we can become fixed and inflexible when we are unreceptive to change, a recipe for misfortune when approaching the world with flexibility is essential for longevity.

It is important to acknowledge and respect our conditionings; however, if they become the only guiding forces for our actions and undertakings, they can lead to the limitation of inflexibility and in turn, our movement away from longevity.

When our minds become too attached to things, they naturally become fixed, just like ice. Ice can crack. This can present a large problem when we are dealing with life challenges we hope to overcome. Oftentimes, solutions to our challenges will rest and depend on our openness to cultivate a flexible mind, something made in the likeness of water. Water is flexible in that it flows in all directions and is not attached to flowing one way. It emulates the concept of longevity. By becoming like water, we are able to let go of our attachments so we can deal with our life challenges, increasing our longevity.

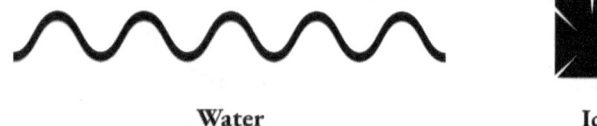

Water   Ice

For people in the U.S., a way to embrace flexibility could be to release our attachments to ultra-processed foods and unhealthily prepared foods. It is becoming common knowledge that excess consumption of ultra-processed foods and unhealthily prepared food can be detrimental to our health, of-tentimes being carcinogenic and increasing chronic disease risk.

While it is true that in the U.S. there is a prevalence of communities with limited grocery stores and an oversaturation of fast-food restaurants, and there are copious amounts of salt being added to our food to enhance flavor (which motivates us to continue eating the unhealthy food), it is also true that we have cultural and social attachments to these foods that tie us to them. Some people cannot imagine a world that does not include hanging out with friends eating ultra-processed foods from their favorite fast-food restaurants.

Similarly, in the African American community, there is a strong attachment to the significance of soul food being food of the culture, food made with love, and food that provides a testament to a people's ability to create a traditional cuisine out of the dark times of slavery and persecution. Eating this food was a survival technique that involved expressing great flexibility and ingenuity for the times people were living in.

Even so, today many fast-food restaurants and soul food meals include large portions of deep-fried dishes made with meat, fat, sugar, and salt, which can increase the risk of obesity, heart disease, type 2 diabetes, dementia, and cancer. Living with flexibility might involve modifying the preparation methods of these foods to make them healthy or modifying dietary habits altogether.

We have to be able to acknowledge the positive memories and attachments associated with these foods and also be able to call timeout. There is a problem of mothers, fathers, aunts, and uncles dying too young and hurting from chronic diseases known to be caused by the habitual consumption of unhealthy ingredients and foods. Family experiences of death and pain from such diseases are a reality we all hope can change.

We may say we want healthier communities, want to build more generational wealth, or want to enjoy more years with close family; however, our attachments to maintaining detrimental social behaviors and cultural norms can be or seem stronger than these desires. In turn, our inability to let go of our attachments and become flexible can easily become what perpetuates the cause of the very problems we hope to remedy. When we hold too tightly onto ideas that were meant to guide us in the past, it is difficult to move forward freely into progress. This is why it is said that attachment is blinding.

∞∞∞

Cultivating a flexible mind and learning not to let my attachments be the only guiding force in my life were essential to dealing with conflict associated with various aspects of my journey. It was only when I began to let go of attachments that we was able to develop a flexible mind, which allowed me to live in harmony with the law of longevity.

As the weeks passed in the hospital, my family had a choice to continue trying increased doses of different anti-inflammatory drugs or have an operation on my gastrointestinal tract. The attachment to my family's preconceived negative ideas about surgery was guiding us in the direction of continuing the drug route; however, my personal history was showing that this might be a futile effort.

By loosening the grip of our attachments and refusing to let them be the sole guiding force for our decisions, my family became flexible and able to act in harmony with the principles that support longevity. Surgery was the route we chose, and by exercising flexibility to move both left and right, towards drugs and towards surgery, I made it out of the conflict I was experiencing at the hospital.

If we had remained fixed and attached to our dislikes of surgery, even considering the changing circumstances in the hospital that became more medically severe, I could have moved closer to collapsing just like a stiff tree up against strong winds.

Out of the hospital, cultivating flexibility continued to be a beneficial focus that would align me with the universe's law of longevity. The ability to eat any food I wanted was a fresh experience for me after my surgeries, because while in the hospital I could not adequately absorb nutrients and was dependent on intravenous nutrition. Occasionally I was able to eat; however, my hospital meal selection was usually limited to milk-based protein shakes.

For the first time in what felt like forever, I could eat what I wanted since I was out of the hospital, so I primarily ate foods that were culturally valued and socially normal. This included foods more common to the Standard American Diet (SAD). While I did enjoy the ability to eat foods my family and peers were eating, I also knew that I never wanted to go through the same severe health experience I had gone through in the hospital.

This meant I needed to better understand the determinants of both positive and negative health outcomes. I found food to be a leading influence on health outcomes. This conclusion led me to a crossroads, where I was tasked with deciding between maintaining my attachments to my cultural eating habits, including my SAD diet, or letting go of the great control the attachments had on me.

In alignment with my ambitious goal at the time, which was to be as healthy as I could, I followed the path of flexibility and loosened attachments to my cultural and social customs so they would not be the only forces directing my eating habits. By doing this, I was introduced to a whole new world of health that involved the adoption of intentional eating habits that positively supported my health. I modified my diet by decreasing my sodium and sugar intake, eating more cooked whole foods, and reducing my consumption of processed foods.

In addition to the flexibility to adopt different eating habits, I experienced great benefits by being open to seeing the world from a different point of view, one that consisted of the notion that all life events were classrooms meant to help teach me something and grow me into a better person.

Previously, I was attached to the notion that life happened without a rhyme or reason, a view that that could leave my life feeling devoid of purpose. From my new perspective, however, everything in life served a purpose and could help me along my own personal journey of self-development if I was open to growing. This was a conscious effort to let go of my attachment to old ideas and something that aligned me with the principles of longevity because successfully navigating life's classrooms involved having the flexibility to embrace personal growth.

∞∞∞

As with the cyclical nature of seasons, life is flexible and is constantly in flux. It is the movement between spring, summer, fall, and winter or between wet and dry seasons that sustains existence. If nature was inflexible and became stuck in only one season, all of life would be unnatural. It is the ability to change that is essential to life's progression, and so too flexibility is an important guiding principle for our own lives.

Can we remain firm in character, yet flexible? Yes. Flexibility does not represent the absence of discipline. We can still be disciplined and committed to flexibility through self-reflection and adaptability.

A great source of error in our lives can be characterized by an inflexible mind. However, when we consciously embrace flexibility in all aspects of our lives and learn to let go of our attachments, whether they be our attachments to emotional states, lifestyles, ideas, customs, or fulfilling our desires, we can progress through life in a way that align us with longevity.

Living with emotional flexibility can allow us to let go of attachments that prevent us from experiencing joy. Intellectual flexibility can allow us to let go of attachments that prevent us from learning and benefiting from diverse knowledge from around the world or from right down the street. Flexibility to let go attachments to our desires can help us learn to better value and do more with less. The examples can continue, but the essence will be the same. A flexible mind combined with a disciplined character can help us not get stuck in our ways and help us live in harmony with the nature of an ever-changing world.

By embracing flexibility in all aspects of our lives, we can be more like any flexible tree, something that is able to bend and not break no matter how hard the winds of life blow. *"Embracing flexibility nourishes our lives."*

PUTTING IT INTO PRACTICE

- *Let go of your attachments to things.*

- *Practice being flexible in your thinking.*

- *Be open to change.*

- *Avoid extremes and find the middle path in life.*

- *Do what seems natural in the environment and time in which you are living.*

8

Breath

*Taking deep breaths helps us become
masters of our lives.*

Anger can propel us to act rapidly and unintentionally tense up. Joy might move us to act
with an outgoing spirit and dance. Worry can move
us to act in a restless manner and become withdrawn. Grief might move us to act with lethargy and
become numb.

Whatever the emotions are, they all share a
common ability, the power to "move" us to act a particular way, oftentimes automatically. The word
"emotion" is derived from "emovere," a Latin word
that means "to move" or "to stir up." There are times
in life when automatic responses driven by emotions
are called for; however, in excess, they can end up
controlling too much of our lives.

Overcoming conflict requires being intentional about how we live. Alternatively, allowing our emotions to control our actions limits our ability to live with intention. I experienced limitations created by emotions in my health journey. However, I also gained personal freedom from the controlling power of emotions when I began to focus on taking deep breaths.

Emotions are not just some made-up notions about what's going on in someone's mind. In actuality, they are a faculty within our lives that serves as a powerful force and something that represents a very real and measurable physiological state within our bodies. When we perceive a stressful situation, are in a constant state of stress, or are emotionally aroused, the chemical makeup of our body changes due to the release of many chemical substances. This can include hormones and neurotransmitters, chemical substances that affect our body metabolism, all the way to how we act day to day.

In a state of stress, blood vessels narrow, and our blood becomes filled with the chemical substance cortisol. Similar to how stress can change the chemistry of our body, emotions like anger, joy, worry, grief, fear, and pleasure can all do the same. The body produces, but is not limited to producing, adrenaline when there is anger, serotonin when there is joy, cortisol when there is worry, grief, or fear, and dopamine when there is pleasure. During all forms of emotional arousal, our breathing patterns also change. Learning to regulate our breathing provides a pathway to regulating emotions.

The magical force of emotions can also influence other aspects of our lives. It can impact our actions, recalibrate our health, affect our cognitive capabilities, and invigorate or depress our energy levels. We can see these effects all play out in our own lives.

In heavy traffic we might see someone get angry and then make an abrupt, rash action like honking their horn or tailgating the car in front of them. Additionally, the 24-hour news cycle might detail unsettling current events, leaving us feeling anxious and soon finding ourselves taking an action that releases this emotion, like working out or binge eating. This stress and anxiety is often accompanied by more rapid breathing.

In school, students tend to get sick near final exam week, something that appears to have a positive correlation with the overwhelming stress they are experiencing. Their breathing patterns are likely to be tight or restricted during this period of stress. The opposite can occur for people recovering from an illness, where a positive correlation can often be seen between being happy and experiencing an increase in health. In this case, breathing is likely to be open and free. This is why in many traditional healing practices, emotions and breathing are directly related to the overall health picture of a patient, and why it is held that health can drop and susceptibility to disease can increase from excess stress, anger, worry, grief, and fear.

We can see an example of our cognitive ability fluctuating during a situation of panic when we are looking for a misplaced wallet. As the time without the wallet increases, our stress levels heighten, and we forget that we handed it to a friend to hold. Stress led our memory and concentration to decrease and while running around looking for the wallet, our breathing pattern likely became tense.

When we hear heavy news or experience traumatic events, we might find ourselves stressing out, getting worried or depressed, and sighing or holding our breath without noticing while our energy levels decrease in unison with the onset of these emotions. Alternatively, when we hear positive news, we can find ourselves joyful with higher energy levels and smoother, deeper breathing.

We may read motivational messages or insightful books; however, when emotions are aroused, they can be what directs our actions if we don't have a superior method of directing our own life force. Similarly, exceptional motivational speakers can have the ability to convey a message that arouses an invigorating emotion that helps move us to accomplish certain goals. However, when the message is finished, other emotions like pleasure or stress might naturally go back to directing our actions, thus creating a dependence on the motivational messages.

For example, say a personal trainer motivated someone not to eat sugary donuts every morning so they could get fit and lower their blood sugar. They felt so motivated by the trainer's messages that they decided to stop eating them until their health improved. But then one morning, they drove by the local donut shop, and saw a sign for a special deal for their favorite donut. Their breathing likely became faster as the emotion of excitement kicked in and drew them to go get those tasty donuts.

Whether it's sweet food, an entertaining location, or a beautiful person, the emotion of pleasure can move us towards things we crave, even if they may not always be beneficial to us. It's not enough to hear information or think about a goal; we must do something that can impact our *will* if we want to intentionally direct our life force.

People who do not have others' best interests in mind exploit the directive power of emotions to control others' actions. They use evocative words, music, videos, or other devices to keep people in a constant state of emotional arousal, providing a breeding ground for emotions to control human behavior. These types of people essentially form an alliance with the emotional aspect of our lives, which can move our *will* into the background; for example, people who fearmonger.

Since, in some way, emotions have the ability to influence our actions, they can act as a pilot, the pilot of our *will*. Nonetheless, we need not remain on autopilot. We have the power to steer towards living intentional and great lives.

There are many ways to cultivate the ability to direct our *will*; however, one effective way that has worked in my journey, and that has been a timeless practice for various cultures around the world, is methodically and intentionally engaging in deep breathing. Unlike emotional arousal, which can be automatic and lead to impulsivity of action or thoughts, deep diaphragmatic breathing is an intentional process. This type of breathing involves expanding and contracting the belly, instead of the chest, with each breath.

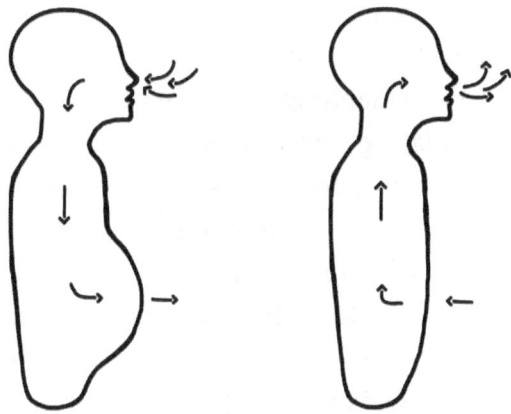

Since our breathing patterns automatically change when our emotions are aroused, the act of intentionally breathing can work to regulate our breath, an otherwise automatic process that would be influenced by mental or emotional tension. Thus, deep breathing can serve as our conscious effort to regain the natural pattern of breath so that it is slow and rhythmic. In terms of simplified brain anatomy and physiology, it is the limbic system that can regulate the connection between emotions and breathing.

By engaging in deep rhythmic breathing, we not only involve ourselves in a process that would normally be automatic during emotional arousal, but also address the physiological state that our bodies are under during this tension. This happens for many reasons, one of which is because the hormones and neurotransmitters that are released during emotional arousal can be reduced or balanced when we engage in deep diaphragmatic breathing.

Regulating our breathing so we can think from a clear headspace can also help us better recognize that we are not required to follow the suggested actions that arise in our minds during emotional arousal. These are thoughts that arise out of impulse rather than an expression of our intentional, internal thinking process. For example, when aroused by fear or worry, we may think, "I am worthless; I should quit." At these times it is important to remember we are not our emotions or thoughts. We have the ability to choose what we are moved to do.

By exercising our freedom of choosing whether to follow or ignore our impulses, we nourish our formless self, whose identity is not associated with these impulses.

Our breath is important, and engaging in intentional deep breathing practices can offer the opportunity to consciously control the actions, health outcomes, mental processes, and energy levels that are influenced by the force of emotions.

∞∞∞∞

Stress and emotional arousal can be common experiences for people dealing with severe health conditions. There are many unknowns, and no day is ever the same.

Although I did not practice deep breathing consistently and methodically until a few years after the zenith of my health journey, when I looked back at entries from a journal I kept throughout this turbulent time, I noticed I wrote that deep breathing helped me live more intentionally. I suffered great, self-imposed emotional tension from the distance I existed away from my desire to live a "normal" life at the time. My behavior, health, cognitive ability, and energy levels, were all being impacted by this mental and emotional tension.

When I worried throughout my health journey, I acted in a mentally restless way where I constantly thought about the future, and I was moved to crave salty and sugary foods and snacks.

When I was stressed out or overly anxious, I experienced a direct connection to a decrease in my digestive health. I would have to spend more hours in the bathroom those days and wouldn't absorb as much of the food I ate compared to days when I had less stress.

In ninth grade, when I eventually returned to school in person four months after my final surgery, I found that my cognitive abilities to focus and concentrate in class were diminished whenever I was stressed, angry, or anxious about the frequency of my digestive elimination throughout the day. During days when I engaged in deep breathing to maintain a calm demeanor, my cognitive abilities remained level.

Lastly, whenever I became depressed or wallowed in my mental disaffection with life, my energy level would feel lower, while my energy level felt much higher on the days when I was more joyful, willfully found gratitude for all aspects of life, and focused on breathing intentionally.

For me, deep breathing greatly helped me deal with the conflict I was experiencing because it helped me better control the force of emotions. The moments where I took deep breaths during intense emotional arousal helped me better control my behavior by slowing down the automatic impulse for me to freeze, like a deer in headlights, from my constant worry and craving specific foods; it helped to slightly slow down my digestion by decreasing my stress levels throughout the day; improved my ability to focus in class by calming me down regardless of the reality of me needing to leave classes often; and helped decrease my feelings of stress and depression so that I could be filled with more joy and gratitude, giving me higher energy levels throughout the day.

The more that I engaged in deep breathing, the better I could navigate the conflict associated with my health journey because I had a greater opportunity to have an intentional influence on my emotions, which in turn influenced my behavior, health, cognitive functions, and energy levels.

∞∞∞∞

Conflict can often stimulate emotional responses in our lives that lead us to live limited lives, because we do, feel, and think what our emotions tell us. However, we can empower ourselves to transcend the limitations created by the force of emotions by using the tool of deep breathing.

Although emotions can be powerful, they are not inherently bad; they are simply a force and something that we might better control through deep diaphragmatic breathing. And, since they are a force, we can benefit from ensuring they don't serve as the main source that directs our lives.

By recognizing the powers of emotions, we might even be able to utilize them to help us better achieve our goals. For example, instead of allowing emotional pleasure to impulsively move us to pursue entertainment every afternoon, we can intentionally experience pleasure for pursuing our New Year's resolution to spend our afternoons getting exercise.

This way, we do not allow the emotional force to un-consciously guide us. Instead, we control this force, something that might heighten our attraction to things, and use it so that it aids us in achieving our intentional goals. Regulating our breath can help us in this effort to better control the actions we are moved to take.

In moments of profound stress or emotional arousal, we can lean on our ability to breathe deeply to engage in the process of regulating our own lives and not let them be regulated unconsciously. For many of us who live with excessive stress or emo-tional tension (e.g., experiencing a health challenge, living in a dangerous environment, or navigating fi-nancial hardship), we can still benefit from engaging in deep breathing during the day and do not have to wait for our emotions to boil up before we try to breathe deeply.

Anytime the force of emotions tries to auto-matically affect our behavior, health, mind, or energy levels in some way, we can regulate it by deeply breathing so that we can act from a higher faculty of our mind that can decide whether our emotional impulse is aligned with reason or is strictly spontaneous. By concentrating on our breathing throughout the day so that it becomes nat-urally deep and rhythmic, we create an opportunity to become the pilot in command of the powerful emotional force that steers our *will*. *"Taking deep breaths helps us become masters of our lives."*

PUTTING IT INTO PRACTICE

- *Engage in deep, diaphragmatic breathing throughout the day.*

- *Concentrate on your breath and deepen your breathing when you are experiencing heightened emotions.*

- *Notice when your actions, health, cognitive functions, and energy levels fluctuate by observing your breathing patterns and emotional state.*

- *Ponder whether your thoughts are coming from a clear headspace or emotional fluctuation and exercise your personal freedom to follow or ignore the thoughts.*

- *Slow and deepen your breathing to give birth to the pilot of your will.*

9

Value

Our outer world reflects the values we have cultivated within ourselves.

For a tree to grow healthy and tall, it needs strong roots. Without a supreme focus on developing below earth's surface, trees cannot effortlessly ascend upwards above the surface.

It is by directing a considerable effort towards the unseen aspects of its form that the seen aspects of trees can better navigate life above the ground. Changing seasons, storms, and cold days can make up life. Although these can sometimes seem like uneasy times, the trees' effort to grow roots helps them thrive through the changes in nature. Similar to how a tree develops great roots and becomes better at living through the changing seasons of life, developing value within myself helped me grow inner roots that let me better live through the difficulty of my journey.

The emphasis on growing something that is unseen or below a surface can appear puzzling, as many of us are conditioned to look only at the outer appearance of things. For example, in health we might look at outer appearances of the body and not inquire about someone's emotional health. However, it is emotional health that can easily dictate the functions of the body.

In another example we might look at the outer spectacle of a house and overlook the internal space that is its makeup, even though the rooms of a house are what make it a useful space for living. Although the inner is often ignored, sometimes even seeming irrelevant, it is truly what helps give function to the outer form of things.

Our personal lives follow the same formula. The skills of esteemed athletes that are witnessed in great arenas were refined during time away, where they focused on perfecting their craft and laying the foundation for a life where their goals can be achieved. From within themselves, they mentally settled on a goal to become the best athletes they could, and this internal value then served as a guide that directed their life actions.

Rooted by the guiding force of their inner value, they might eat and sleep a certain way to ensure they have ample energy for their competitions, watch TV or read articles that are relevant and beneficial to their goals, or say "no" to engaging in activities that deviate from their internal values.

All aspects of their outer life are a reflection of the values that they rooted themselves in. Without an established internal value, they could end up being guided by an aimless force, and they might have less strength to navigate the challenges associated with their sport. However, their discipline to develop and live by internal values creates the opportunity for their outer experiences to be a beautiful reflection of their inner values.

For all people, whether they be athletes, students, farmers, or businessmen, growing an internal value is one of the most favorable goals there is. With an inner value, the outer reflection of our lives can become a magnificent display of radiating light.

After weeks of being unable to eat in the hospital, the first food I ate after my surgeries was a bag of my favorite hot, crunchy corn chips. I felt so much joy and satisfaction from eating them. My desire had been fulfilled.

Unfortunately, though, my body did not appreciate this food as I experienced bad stomach cramps and indigestion after consumption. I wanted to change this outer experience of painful health outcomes, and to do this, my first step was to look within and develop an internal value. For me, it was during this time that my roots grew as I developed an internal value to be healthy.

After all the pain and hardship I had just gone through, I declared that I loved what remained of my digestive tract too much to indulge in the temporary pleasures of tasty, unhealthy food that would only cause me long-term suffering. This experience enlightened me about the importance of cultivating internal values and living by them. I needed to establish harmony in my life.

Guided by my internal values, I tried to get adequate sleep, embrace slower living, keep a joyful outlook on life, spend time with loved ones, eat whole foods, and keep naturally moving. As time passed, my outer experiences in life were becoming a reflection of my internal value.

Even as the deep roots of this internal value guided many of my actions, my outer experiences still sometimes felt devoid of purpose when I searched for value outside of myself. I looked around, asking, "What should I try to attain or be?" I thought, "Should I become a programmer, doctor, professional athlete, business mogul, or try to pursue fame and power?" The list went on.

Looking outside was an endless and aimless search with no clear answers. This was in part because my severe time in the hospital showed that life is very brief and that even if you pursue the attainment of certain material pleasures, they don't last forever and will always leave you desiring more. Whether it's a millionaire or a pauper, there is only a certain level of medical care available that they can receive when they are ill. Thus, when we are afforded health, it makes sense to live life with the fullest of intention. This realization led to a search for deeper meaning in life and, consequently, a deeper search within.

By meditating to focus my attention on growing something inside myself and diverting it away from solely material things outside of myself, I began living a life where growing roots for becoming a better human was my internal value. When I lived with actions that were in harmony with this internal value, my external world could reflect my internal truth. Answers to questions about where the purpose and value in life were became clearer because I could create this purpose and value by letting it become an extension of what was already inside of me.

My internal value involved honoring peace, love, harmony, and integrity, and it served as the guiding force for how I would live my daily life. To strengthen the roots of my internal value, I would focus on living true to the value at crossroads in life. For example, living truthfully with this value at a crossroads meant treating all things and people from a place of love. Anytime that I transgressed against this value, my roots would shrink in size, making it harder for the values inside of me to manifest outside in life.

Additionally, when I needed to decide whether or not to do something, I could weigh the proposed undertaking as if it were on a scale of judgment. If the proposed action was balanced with my internal values, then I would engage in the activity. If not, I would try to let go of my interest in that activity. For example, if my internal value was to embrace sustainability and that value was placed on one side of the scale, but I was also interested in shopping for unnecessary gadgets and I placed that desire on the other side of the scale, then the scale would become imbalanced. In this case, I would reject the activity of unnecessary shopping. Doing this helped ensure my personal interests or ideas arising from emotional impulses were not the only motivating factors of my actions. Deep internal values were the guiding force. From such a practice of weighing my values and personal interests, making important decisions and creating value outside of my life became easier. My external value was simply an extension of my internal value.

∞∞∞∞

A great challenge can arise for many of us when it seems like there is nothing of importance outside of us to pursue. Maybe in the past we had certain goals and structured our lives around pursuing them, but then everything collapsed, leaving us feeling empty. All that has happened is that the outer aspect of our lives is trying to traverse the changing seasons on its own. It cannot do this well without the guidance of our roots. The next step is for us to go within; just like trees that pull their nutrients inwards during the cold times of winter, we should direct our focus inwards and nurture our inner values.

When a seed is first placed in the ground, it grows its roots and connects with the soil before it emerges from the ground. For trees, the unseen and inward quality can be likened to their roots, and for us humans, the unseen can be likened to our hearts and minds.

When the internal values we establish are intended to make us better humans, we can begin to create wonderful situations outside of our lives that reflect the abundant qualities of peace, love, joy, and harmony that are truly established from within and not from the external or material world. We should seek the kingdom within.

Without growing internal values, we can experience the more challenging effects of a non-purposeful life experience; however, by cultivating value within ourselves, everything we do can be with purpose. We can eat, listen to music, form relationships or communities, and work with purpose. We can then experience purposeful living, like great leaders whose entire lives are rooted in their internal values.

By living with an all-encompassing focus on purpose, our lives can become a grand push upwards towards our greatest potential and highest good, where our lives become a reflection of what we already established and grew within ourselves. *"Our outer world reflects the values we have cultivated within ourselves."*

PUTTING IT INTO PRACTICE

- *Look within yourself for purpose and value, and if you don't find anything, then create it.*

- *Seek activities that are in alignment with your internal values.*

- *Spend time growing and strengthening the roots of your internal values.*

10

Stillness

*Becoming still connects us with a
source of great power.*

G reat masters of their craft often share one
thing in common: the ability to embrace stillness. While performing their forms, a martial artist
stills their mind and body, waiting for the right moment to move. At a recital, a pianist stills their mind
and hands before beginning the performance. A
strategist embraces stillness to have more clarity
when making important decisions. A basketball
player stills their mind and takes a deep breath before shooting the free throw.

In an effort to successfully master different
undertakings, stilling the mind can serve as a pre-
requisite. When it came to dealing with the conflict

of my journey, learning to still my mind helped me become a champion of my difficult undertaking.

Since stillness is a natural mental state that promotes optimal performance of different tasks, it is important to understand how this stillness can be both established and lost. The quality of stillness can be visualized as a lake surrounded by mountains, where the lake's water either sits or flows calmly.

This stillness is lost when lightning strikes or strong winds blow upon the water, causing it to begin to rapidly move. This change in stillness is not always a bad thing. When it is natural for the water to move somewhere, the wind and lightning might assist this process; however, if there is constant work done by the wind and lightning onto the lake, then the water will always crash around, and the water's ability to remain still or flow in a specific direction might be impeded.

In our lives, this lake filled with water can be likened to our minds, wind can be stimuli, and lightning can be our thoughts. Anytime our mind is introduced to stimuli like images or sounds, the stillness that existed changes as we might focus on the whirlwind of stimuli. Similarly, anytime we are engaged in constant thinking, the stillness in our minds has also transformed because our thoughts work like a force, just like the force of lightning upon a lake.

In the life of a martial artist competing in a sparring match, the strong wind might be words from an opponent or distracting banners in the crowd. The lightning might be a mind that constantly strikes with questions like, "What if I make a mistake?" or "What is everybody thinking?" Without taking measures to control the *weather* (the wind and lightning), the state of their mind will reflect a turbulent lake, and it will be harder to execute their martial arts efficiently.

Additionally, if their mind loses its stillness, the opponent would have already won the match. With an overstimulated mind, the martial artist introduces an additional opponent to the arena and loses via self-sabotage. The same applies whether we are competing in a martial arts competition, taking an exam, performing in front of an audience, or undergoing a new challenge.

However, by bending with the wind and focusing the lightning strikes of their thoughts in a healthy direction, the martial artist can direct their mind. This could look like zoning their hearing and sight onto the task at hand and dropping their thinking so they become present with the moment and all their thoughts can relate to their important body movements. They know that to defeat someone you must first defeat them in the mind, and so the martial artist takes measures to first bring stillness to their mind.

Just as strong winds aren't always present in the sky, swaying sounds and images aren't always present in our lives, meaning that there are times when outside stimuli aren't trying to affect our mind in a disruptive way. However, our thoughts, just like the lightning, might be more powerful influences when they occur, because they force a higher concentrated energy burst on the environment.

Both lightning and our thoughts can arise quickly and can cause a jolt in their environments, whether it be the lake's water or the stillness of our mind. To establish stillness, it is ideal for fewer strong winds and lightning to be constantly affecting the lake of our mind.

There are many ways to control the *weather* within our minds; however, some valuable methods can involve creating calmness in our environment to control the wind and meditating to control the lightning. If we are constantly being stimulated by entertainment, negative images, pessimistic rhetoric, or intoxicating substances, these outside agents can easily affect the internal stillness of our minds, disrupt the lake, and disempowers our lives. This can in turn impact our ability to achieve goals or over-come conflict that would otherwise require a still mind. So, by being intentional about what stimuli are imposed onto our minds and bodies, we can control the wind so as to create an opportunity for stillness. Doing so empowers our lives.

By meditating, we can embrace a natural state of mind that is absent of perpetual thought. If we were to be thinking all the time and about different things, the lightning would be forcing the lake's water to constantly be thrust in all sorts of directions. We might find ourselves creating this lightning while perpetually thinking things such as, "Should I do this or that?" "Am I up to the task?" "Do they like me?" or "Am I doing enough?" All the while, we might simply just be trying to clean the dishes.

Intentional thinking and joyfully visualizing a reality we hope to experience is an auspicious way to utilize our minds. Additionally, by letting go of all of our thoughts and embracing inner silence through meditation, we can control the powerful lightning and allow our mind to be still. As a wise person once said, "Stop thinking and end your problems."

Conflict and uncertainty were natural occurrences that arose in my life when I first entered the hospital. Every hour I could hear various beeping alarm sounds from the medical equipment attached to my body, with the rhythm and pitch of the sounds sometimes changing. I would lose blood nearly every hour in a painful and uncomfortable way with my sleep schedule being nonexistent most days. I often saw different-colored fluid coming out of my body or entering my body through an IV and would spend hours in anticipation waiting for the doctors to share updates on my prognosis.

Needless to say, I found myself in a place where it was natural to have thoughts like, "There is no way out of this circumstance," "The ability to overcome this challenge isn't at all in my hands," and "Can this all just please change?" Feeling blown away by the stressful environment and struck by the thoughts of doubt, confusion, and anxiety, I knew that I needed to find a place of peace to make it through this conflict. I needed to enter the stillness.

To balance out the stressful environment that was stimulating my mind to become restless, like a lake that is constantly developing strong currents by the forceful wind, I asked for a Bluetooth speaker as a holiday gift so I could play calming music. Inspired by the therapeutic ambiance I felt while getting acupuncture treatments prior to being hospitalized, I played the same music playlist that was always played in the acupuncture room. All day and every day I listened to peaceful music, which effectively created an environment that was more still and meditative.

Not only did this help promote stillness in my mind, but it likely did for the nurses, interns, and doctors, as they would constantly share how calm and rejuvenated they felt whenever they entered my hospital room. Additionally, I took time away from social media by deleting the apps on my phone, and I limited my media consumption. Whenever I did watch different media, I watched programs related to more positive or joyful things. In this way, I better controlled the force of the wind.

To balance out my thoughts that were making my mind jump around, like lightning bolts striking water erratically, I began to practice medi-tation. At this time, meditation for me meant a controlled effort to focus my entire thinking in one direction and to engage in deep breathing.

Whenever the nurses or doctors entered my room, I tried to drop my thoughts and give all my at-tention to them. Whenever a family member visited me, I tried to drop my thoughts and focus on our in-teractions. When I was working on school assignments, I would focus all my thoughts on the assignments. When I was sitting in my hospital bed with nothing to do, I would often close my eyes and be present, breathe deeply, and try to just be still, embracing the emptiness of my mind. Other times when lying in my bed, I visualized a fire in my stom-ach, representative of my inflamed colon, beginning to cool down over time while I continued to try and breathe deeply.

Although it was common for my thoughts of confusion and anxiety to jolt me, especially when my pain levels increased, I would try to not entertain these thoughts, and I would let them pass. These practices helped me better control the supercharged lightning. It was the combined effort of becoming a better master of my environment and thoughts that helped me create stillness in my mind. This stillness helped me to be more like other masters of their crafts who cultivate stillness to succeed in whatever undertaking they are going through.

In my case, the stillness I embraced helped me to connect with a greater strength that would carry me through my health conflict in a peaceful manner, where important decisions regarding my health were made from a leveled head, where I could undergo pain or unwanted external situations un-flinchingly, where I could better intuit the reasons behind why I had better digestion certain days com-pared to others (usually relating to my diet, water intake, emotions, or extent of my engagement in physical activities), and where I could view my cir-cumstance from a place of opportunity to learn great life lessons.

Although I was not perfect at embracing a still mind all the time, whenever I practiced these methods of controlling my environment and mind, I would experience the benefits of stillness. I could weather the storm.

∞∞∞∞

What if stillness was our natural state all the time? Would we all be better at navigating any un-dertaking we are going through, no matter how big or small it might be? We all have the opportunity to connect with a great source of power whenever we embody stillness.

It is the stillness of mind that offers us the ability to attain supreme focus on our objectives, see an undertaking through to completion, and ensure our minds aren't distracted by negative thoughts, images, or words that could disrupt our minds' focus. If whatever we think and say can become a reality, why not embrace stillness so we can think and say the positive things we would hope to see in our lives?

Sometimes we may find ourselves scared of this stillness. Our minds might be racing. We might be afraid of how expansive our minds are and have constant stimuli in our environment that always keep us thinking 24/7. However, if we take the leap to let go of the unrest, we may find that we can become better masters of our minds, as we will be embracing the power associated with stillness. By making an effort to change our environments to align them more with serenity and direct our thinking so it becomes quiet and focused, we can live like the other masters out there in the world.

We are constantly going through different life circumstances, all with varying degrees of challenge and opportunity, and the ability to traverse these circumstances can be impacted by the degree of our stillness. For this reason, we can always remember that to master our lives, we first must master our minds, and after mastering our minds, we need not master anything else. Self-mastery is key.

The world is grander than we are and trying to impose our *will* on the world can be a futile effort, as we might not always be able to immediately change our external circumstances, such as the people in our lives or events taking place in our surroundings. Learning to master our minds, however, lets us better navigate life because we can operate from a place of stillness, just like the other masters of their crafts.

People with a formless self-image excel at establishing stillness through mastering their minds. They know their thoughts are not characteristics of their self-image, just as a lake's identity is not mistaken for lightning simply because a storm is passing overhead. *Formless people's* thoughts are a force that is simply passing through their minds. Whenever these thoughts strike from place to place, *formless people* remain still, allowing them to pass by like they were a passing thunderstorm. They learn to let go of their attachment to their passing thoughts and not entertain detrimental thoughts.

When *formless people* pause and breathe deeply during a mental storm, they observe that their thoughts are jumping from place to place. Observing their thoughts lets them clearly see that there is a separation between the observer and the thoughts themselves. By recognizing this separation, *formless people* can better embrace inner stillness even amidst the constant movement of these thoughts in their minds. The observer is the true identity of *formless people*, and they maintain a formless self-image by not identifying with their thoughts. They don't mistake their thoughts or impulses to be their identity.

No matter how sporadic the thoughts become, people with a formless *self-image* simply observe them and let them pass. This way, they can tap into the great power of stillness, which enhances their abilities to master their minds and navigate their life journeys.

With stillness, they can better drop their thinking and expand their *perspectives* to see the fullness of life; center themselves in *gratitude* so they may experience an undisturbed state of peace; expand their inexhaustible inner *joy*; pour their *hearts* into everything to proliferate beauty in life; live with greater patience through life's changing cyclical *seasons*; nourish their ability to be *flexible* so they align with qualities of longevity; enhance their ability to direct their *will* through conscious control of their *breath*; and realize the kingdom of *value* within their hearts. Stillness not only gives them peace, but it also gives them great power. *"Becoming still connects us with a source of great power."*

PUTTING IT INTO PRACTICE

- *Embrace the silence and engage in mindfulness meditation practices.*

- *Do less.*

- *Establish stillness in your environment (e.g., clean your room of any clutter).*

- *Decrease stimuli (e.g., technology) or substances (e.g., foods, drinks, or drugs) that can devitalize your life.*

- *Only entertain thoughts and visualizations about what you want to see happen in your life.*

Afterword

In physics class, I learned the greater the force applied to an object, the greater the force that object applies in return to match it. All forces come in pairs and are equal and opposite. This law also holds true in our personal lives. The greater the force of conflict we experience, the greater the force of power we can harness to match the conflict. These forces are also equal and opposite.

Everything in our life is a part of a grander purpose, and we owe it to ourselves to never give up in the face of personal or worldly challenges. By keeping an unwavering positive spirit, we can harness the equal and opposite power that is available in any given life situation to reestablish harmony.

My lived experiences, readings, and travels to Africa, Europe, and Central America, helped me learn that people all over the world have valuable insights about harmony. I've also found it fascinating that when we make an effort to tap into diverse knowledge and information, we can assemble answers to big questions we have regarding how to experience a healthy life, just like assembling a large multi-piece puzzle.

From the western medical world, the studies of the properties and behavior of matter have allowed doctors and scientists to thoroughly understand the six levels of organization in the human body, including chemical, cellular, tissue, organ, organ system, and organism. This has, in turn, provided a basis for which the intricacies of drugs, surgical procedures, nutritional science, and radiation, among other interventions, have been used to treat irregularities in body function.

In the western medical world, the central term used to describe harmony within the human body is "homeostasis." Homeostasis represents the balance and acceptable range of values for blood pressure, acids, oxygen, proteins, temperature, and others within the body. Our bodies constantly regulate the balance of their internal environments, because when homeostasis is lost, irregularities and disease follow.

From Eastern Asia, the medical art of Traditional Chinese Medicine (TCM) has been brought to the world. Its medical philosophy is centered around promoting harmony within people's lives by establishing the balance of energy, namely the Three Treasures: Jing, Qi, and Shen. Jing is the category of energy that represents the ancestral energy that we inherit from our parents, which is influenced by our genetics; Qi is the category of energy that represents the life force, which can be influenced by things such as our environment, diet, or lifestyle; and lastly, Shen is the category of energy that represents our spirit, which is influenced by the connection between our heart and mind.

TCM philosophy views all diseases as the imbalance of the Three Treasures, and to reestablish the balance of these energies in someone's life, practitioners use tools such as acupuncture, herbs, dietary recommendations, and meditation. Overall, the medical teachings from TCM emphasize that the natural balance and free flow of energy are essential for the manifestation of health.

A medical theory that likely existed for thousands of years and was more recently shared with the rest of the world by European physicians is the "Law of Similars," which is the foundation of homeopathic medicine. This law holds that the same substance that causes disease symptoms in a healthy individual can heal an unhealthy individual living with the same disease symptoms (e.g., someone with a certain type of skin inflammation who describe their symptoms/disease as feeling like their skin is "boiling" will be administered a remedy that can cause the same skin inflammation and sensation in a healthy person).

"Vital force" is the term used in homeopathic medicine to denote the energy that freely circulates the body, and disease is viewed as the result of disturbed and unharmonious flow of this vital force. To address poor health, homeopathic practitioners will follow the Law of Similars to identify substances in nature that can help reestablish the harmony and free flow of vital force.

Upon learning more about world medicine, I was also introduced to a traditional southern African medical theory. Something I found interesting was that from the KwaZulu-Natal province, the word "lungisa" is used as a means of saying "to correct" or "to put in order." Among the traditional Zulu healers in this region, "lungisa" serves as a foundational approach for establishing health. In their medical philosophy, great health and order are represented by the manifestation of positive situations, a healthy environment related to an individual, and a healthy body.

Similarly, many traditional villages in Africa have medicine people, healers who integrate physical health with spirituality through their interconnected worldview. For example, if a medicine woman or man helps heal a family whose son has malaria, it wouldn't be enough for the family to simply know that their son was bitten by a mosquito and he succumbed to malaria. They want to understand why their son got sick and not someone else's son, considering mosquitoes bite many people. With an integrative worldview, where the health of body and spirit are connected, the medicine people maintain the answers to such a question lie in the spiritual realm, and it's addressed through traditional healing interventions.

All these global medical philosophies share a connection, which is that the essence of health is an expression of harmony within our lives. With this in mind, we would do well to recognize and abide by the common understanding that living with greater harmony in our lives will help to reestablish a healthy life experience for us all. We can empower ourselves to take ownership of rebalancing our mind, body, and spirit. Whenever we are met with conflict, we can always look to where harmony can be reestablished so we can overcome the challenges we face.

By reading the 10 meditations presented in the book and seeing real-life examples of their manifestation in my own journey, I hope you will feel that you have at your fingertips a source of light that could help you navigate your journey and reestablish harmony within your life.

Nevertheless, while it is beneficial to read different and insightful literature or hear motivating words, these things alone cannot establish harmony in our lives. What makes a master a master is not the fact that they have read 10,000 books or practiced a skill 10,000 times in the past. It is the fact that they actively try to execute what they have learned and practiced. Similarly, the meditations in this book are not a golden ticket, where reading them once creates perfect harmony in life. They each represent a focus, a meditation that we can intentionally and consistently put into thought and action.

Intentionally putting life meditations into practice and letting go of the things that keep us from transforming delivers us from any conflict we are experiencing and lets us create a beautiful life where we can live in a peaceful and purposeful way. We all have the opportunity to make this a reality.

We should honor the value of personal, intentional effort, as it is how we choose to deal with any hardship in our life that becomes our destiny. So let us create our own destiny and choose to live life with peace and purpose.

Disharmony   **Harmony**   **Disharmony**

The 10 Meditations

For further insight and practice with the content discussed in the book, below you'll find simple exercises I've found helpful in applying the 10 meditations. At the start of each day or week, you can plan to meditate on and try to implement the lessons from one of the 10 meditations. The meditation you choose to focus on can then serve as your guiding focus for that day or week.

1. *Self-image*	2. *Perspective*
3. *Gratitude*	4. *Joy*
5. *Heart*	6. *Seasons*
7. *Flexibility*	8. *Breath*
9. *Value*	10. *Stillness*

Meditation 1 | Self-image

"A formless self-image expands the possibilities in our lives."

- Recreate and redefine your "self-image" to become formless.
- Know that you aren't limited by your past or pedigree. They might be influences on your life, but they aren't the essence of who you are.

- Think about the words you say or think after saying "I am" and ask yourself if these words create a limitation in your life.
- Speak, think, and live in a way that embraces the limitlessness of a formless self-image.

Use formless phrases:

- "I am experiencing sickness."
- "This body is experiencing pain."
- "I am experiencing difficulties with the subject of math and will continue to study to improve."
- "I am experiencing anger/depression/sadness."
- "I've devoted considerable time to athletics. Currently, I am experiencing challenges while trying to do ___."

Avoid permanency phrases and actions:

- "I am sick" or "I am in pain."
- "I am not good at math, but I will continue to study so that I can improve."
- "I am angry/depressed/sad."
- "I am just an athlete. I'm not good at ___."
- "I can't ___" or "I am a bad ___."
- "We've never done those things."

- "That's just how it will be for people like me."
- Repeating sentences that enforce the ideas "I am my past," "I am my disease," "I am my trauma," or "I am my emotions."
- Repeating song lyrics or watching media that re-iterate a sense of self-image permanency.

Meditation 2 | Perspective

"Our perspective gives us the power to fully control our experience of life."

- Choose your own experience of life.
- Let go of ideas and concepts that limit you to seeing life from a fixed/dual point of view (e.g., good or bad).
- Practice thinking and speaking from a non-dual point of view.
- Look at life circumstances and events as opportunities.

Meditation 3 | Gratitude

"Gratitude brings us back to our original undisturbed state of peace."

- Reflect on the day and write down 1-5 things you are grateful for before bed each night.
- Let go of your untamed desires and accept life as it comes.
- Practice letting gratitude become the natural state of your mind.
- Find appreciation for simple things.

Meditation 4 | Joy

"Being joyful lets us fly through life."

- Practice trying to naturally experience joy for life itself.
- Let go of your heavy emotional load so you can become light, spread your wings of joy, and fly.
- Smile, laugh, and spread positivity to others.
- Remember, "Life is too short to be dead serious all the time; smile."

Meditation 5 | Heart

"Whatever you pour your heart into can become something beautiful."

- Pour your heart into everything.
- Practice trying to see the value of everything in life.
- Live with great passion and enthusiasm.

Meditation 6 | Seasons

"Everything in life goes through cycles, and each part of every cycle serves a purpose."

- Relax your mind and trust the natural flow of life's cycles.
- Practice trying to recognize the importance of all seasons in life.
- Practice patience.

Meditation 7 | Flexibility

"Embracing flexibility nourishes our lives."

- Let go of your attachments to things.
- Practice being flexible in your thinking.
- Be open to change.

- Avoid extremes and find the middle path in life.
- Do what seems natural in the environment and time in which you are living.

Meditation 8 | Breath

"Taking deep breaths helps us become masters of our lives."

- Engage in deep, diaphragmatic breathing throughout the day.
- Concentrate on your breath and deepen your breathing when you are experiencing heightened emotions.
- Notice when your actions, health, cognitive functions, and energy levels fluctuate by observing your breathing patterns and emotional state.
- Ponder whether your thoughts are coming from a clear headspace or emotional fluctuation, and exercise your personal freedom to follow or ignore the thoughts.
- Slow and deepen your breathing to give birth to the pilot of your *will*.

Meditation 9 | Value

"Our outer world reflects the values we have cultivated within ourselves."

- Look within yourself for purpose and value, and if you don't find anything, then create it.
- Seek activities that are in alignment with your internal values.
- Spend time growing and strengthening the roots of your internal values.

Meditation 10 | Stillness

"Becoming still connects us with a source of great power."

- Embrace the silence and engage in mindfulness meditation practices.
- Do less.
- Establish stillness in your environment (e.g., clean your room of any clutter).
- Decrease stimuli (e.g., technology) or substances (e.g., foods, drinks, or drugs) that can devitalize your life.
- Only entertain thoughts and visualizations about what you want to see happen in your life.

Simple Daily Meditation Script

Meditation isn't only an ancient science that involves engaging in deep diaphragmatic breathing, bringing stillness to the mind, and sitting in one place for an extended period of time. It can also entail focusing our entire life on whatever is occurring at each moment from a place of deep concentration.

By maintaining this profound focus, every movement we make or word we speak throughout the day turns into a meditation. Subsequently, we emulate an ultimate focus where we harmonize with the present, like a farmer becoming one with the land as they plant the crops or a teacher becoming one with their classroom as they observe the strengths and weaknesses of their students.

At the same time, intentional meditation practices where we dedicate time to stilling our body and mind can be an extremely beneficial focus.

The next few pages provide a simple meditation script. I have followed this script, found it to be rewarding, and would like to share it with you.

<u>Upon waking:</u>

1. Turn on any meditation music (e.g., flute, hand-pan drums, or water sounds) or be one with the silence.

2. Set a 5-to-20-minute timer if just starting out. After some practice, 20 minutes might pass by very quickly; if this occurs, increase the time as you see fit. Additionally, ensure that the timer sound is not a loud alarm sound.

3. Sit comfortably.

4. Relax your shoulders and jaw and rest your hands comfortably on your lap or in any hand position desired.

5. Let your tongue rest at the roof of your mouth and close your eyes.

6. Begin to slowly breathe deeply in through your nose.

7. Slowly breathe out through your nose.

8. Repeat the breathing exercise and let your mind embrace stillness.

9. *Optional: Focus on joyfully visualizing a reality you hope to experience as you continue the meditation.*

10. When the timer expires, slowly open your eyes, and prepare your body for the next task.

Throughout the day:

- Practice becoming aware of your breath by intentionally taking deep, diaphragmatic breaths.
- Maintain a controlled focus on the present.
- Practice the 10 Meditations.

Before sleeping:

1. Sit comfortably.
2. Relax your shoulders and jaw and rest your hands comfortably on your lap or in any hand position desired.
3. Let your tongue rest at the roof of your mouth and close your eyes.
4. Begin to slowly breathe deeply in through your nose.
5. Slowly breathe out through your nose and count "1 breath."
6. Repeat this breathing pattern, gradually working your way up to "20 breaths" or any target you set over time.
7. If you lose track of what number you are on, start back over at 0 and begin the breathing technique again.
8. After completing all the breaths, sit still for some time (10 seconds or longer).

9. *Optional: Focus on joyfully visualizing a reality you hope to experience as you continue the meditation.*

10. Afterwards, slowly open your eyes and prepare your body for the next task.

Meditation...

Q: What should I expect?
A: Nothing, just keep breathing. Just be.

Q: What should I do if my mind
won't stop thinking?
A: Nothing, just keep breathing. Just be.

About the Author

Photo credit: Josiah Finley

Winston A. Wardlaw grew up in Washington, D.C., where he enjoyed spending time with family, drawing, learning Tae Kwon Do, and playing soccer with his brother and close friends. He graduated from North Carolina Agricultural and Technical State University with a B.S. in Food and Nutritional Sciences, and he is currently studying to attain a professional doctorate in Acupuncture and Chinese Herbal Medicine.

Winston has been intimately connected with health since he was a child, and at age 13, when he experienced the debilitating effects of the chronic disease ulcerative colitis, he embarked on a transformative journey. He has spent years observing masters of conventional and ancient healing arts and has gained empirical, lived opportunities to apply profound life lessons. These early-life experiences have been central to overcoming the conflict of his health journey, attaining greater personal health, and creating harmony in his life.

Some of his notable achievements include speaking on the National Mall as the Honored Hero for the Crohn's and Colitis Foundation and becoming a Lewis and Elizabeth Dowdy Scholar, working at the National Institutes of Health (NIH) and in Silicon Valley, and co-founding a production company, Muscle n Bone, LLC, that has published an educational math app (Minute by Minute) and two video games (Hoops n Brickz and Tap n Score).

However, Winston's greatest joys include spending invaluable quality time with loved ones, supporting the efforts of community farmers, playing soccer and basketball with friends, spending time in nature, learning about the empowering effects of meditation and self-knowledge, and being able to live with greater peace and purpose.

Winston's goals are to consistently put the 10 Meditations into practice and to help create a world that reflects greater harmony and light.

www.winstonwardlaw.com

About the Cover

The image on the cover of this book is a photo I took of the Sahara Desert sunrise on my smartphone. I captured this picture while studying abroad in Morocco during a two-day trip to Merzouga, a village in the southeastern desert region of the country.

Historically, the village was a common stop for travelers on the road to Timbuktu. Presently, Merzouga is home to people of Amazigh ethnic origin and is a picturesque location for international travelers.

After sunrise we traveled to Khamlia, a village just a few miles south of Merzouga where people of Gnawa ethnic origin live. At this desert village, I was able to hear the Gnawa tribe's traditional, rhythmic music that has been preserved and passed down from their ancestors in the Sahel region of Africa. They sang memorable songs and played sacred instruments.

The light from the east woke up everything that was slumbering. The sunrise felt like a blanket over the earth as it warmed and lit the cool, dark desert floor. The sunrise radiated beauty and brought light to the land.

www.ingramcontent.com/pod-product-compliance
Lightning Source LLC
Chambersburg PA
CBHW021639120626
46545CB00002B/625